Fix Your Partner
in 10 Easy Steps or Less!

Train Your Partner to Treat You Better

Marlon Familton, MA, LMHC

10 Publishing

Fix Your Partner in 10 Easy Steps or Less!
Train your partner to treat you better
Marlon Familton, MA, LMHC
Copyright © 2015 by Marlon Familton

10 Steps Publishing, Bellevue, WA 98004
Published in the United States of America

Publisher's Cataloging-In-Publication Data
(Prepared by The Donohue Group, Inc.)

Names: Familton, Marlon.
Title: Fix your partner in 10 easy steps or less! : train your partner to treat you better / Marlon Familton, MA, LMHC.
Other Titles: Fix your partner in ten easy steps or less!
Description: First edition. | Bellevue, WA : 10 Steps Publishing, 2015.
Identifiers: ISBN 978-0-692-39400-7 | ISBN 978-0-692-71742-4 (ebook)
Subjects: LCSH: Interpersonal communication. | Interpersonal conflict.
Classification: LCC BF637.C45 F36 2015 (print) | LCC BF637.C45 (ebook) | DDC 153.6--dc23

First Edition, 2015

What others are saying about this book

"A marvelous tool for understanding relationships and communication. If you're looking for a way to stop the roller coaster, or to connect with a partner who doesn't seem to understand what intimacy means, Familton's 'Fix Your Partner in 10 Easy Steps or Less' is a wonderful way to start the conversations every couple must have."

C. Preston LMFT

"Don't be deceived by the lightness of the humor - Marlon Familton captures key messages from findings of the most valuable research on marriage in the past 25 years, especially John Gottman's and Susan Johnson's breakthrough studies, which have helped thousands of couples effectively."

Jennifer Elf, MS, LMHC,
Certified in Gottman Method and EFT Couples Therapy

Fix Your Partner is accessible, informative, and entertaining. Familton manages to provide an understanding of couples attachment styles, meaningful correction to negative communication patterns, and a roadmap to deep and committed relationships. You will love the step-by-step exercises in this book, the scripts for fixing challenging communication patterns, and an insightful new way of perceiving secure relationships. If you are committed to 'fixing' your relationship, this book is for you.

Marianne Marlow, LMHC
Heart Centered Healing Arts

For my wife, Leah . . . for sticking with me when I did it all wrong and giving me multiple chances to do it right.

Everything you do or don't do communicates something to your partner. To have a great relationship be mindful of what you are communicating, always.

Marlon Familton

Contents

About the Author

Marlon Familton is a licensed private practice psychotherapist in Bellevue, Washington, who is focused on helping individuals and couples improve their relationships. He runs Bellevue Family Counseling with his wife, who is a child therapist and parent coach.

After becoming an expert on doing his first marriage wrong and going through a divorce, Marlon went on to get his master's degree in applied behavioral science from Bastyr University. Now he works hard to help his clients build secure and loving relationships as well as keep his second marriage in the "extra special" zone. Marlon can be reached through his websites at www.fixyourpartner.com and www.securelove.net.

Foreword

I met this book's author years and years ago. The same way I found my favorite pizza place. The same way too, I found my best physician, and our perfect place to get away, the same way we all find the best of the best . . . the grapevine. Over and over the name "Marlon Familton" kept coming up in the same context of "the most effective marriage counselor."

Being very curious about him, I called Marlon and that afternoon we met. I immediately appreciated the rational sensibility from which his approach to couples healing and growth came. His ways of understanding marriage were practical and do-able. The feedback I had been getting from clients proved they were also transformational!

I remember the warmth in his eyes, the sincerity too, of his demeanor. I remember thinking he is one of the very few clinicians I'd met in my four decades of clinical practice who talked to me in "human speak". One of the very few who felt no need to hide behind psycho-babble. Instead he spoke with such compassionate, impressively insightful understanding of the common struggles every couple shares. Struggles that took a career for me to comprehend, Marlon discussed so eloquently, as if he'd had direct audio-video feed access to every couple I myself had counseled. I knew then why this man was held in the respectful status his reputation had earned. This was someone special!

Years ago on that day he accepted my invitation to join our

group of counselors. Today that man I'd once sat across from, feeling such respect for, has now has taken the reins of leadership I had once held with our group. A new bar of talent and professionalism, Marlon has set for all of us to now aspire to.

We've all so admired Marlon for the compassion be brings to his role. More so, I continue to hear how his insightful and practical feedback fills the gap that many clients complain lacks in their experience with other counselors. Now in his book, the practical approach and lessons he provides his clients are available to all. These lessons, tools and steps will work. They will restore communication, understanding and trust to your relationship, if you follow them.

Read the book and follow the steps. Marlon will guide your marriage through a communication transformation regardless of your partner's participation. Just remember: this is yours. It is not about them. What your partner will do will be theirs. How you respond will be yours. I know you will enjoy all the benefits that Marlon can offer in the pages that follow. This book will provide you a spectacular opportunity of relationship improvement!

Greg McBride
Author of Finding Your Integrity (2008; McBride)

Acknowledgment

The truth is that I have been sweating over this book since I started working with couples in 2008. The title, the angle, and the content have changed (too) many times, all in an effort to be simple to read and easy to apply. It has taken me so long because it had to be the best I can do. You now hold in your hands the fruit of my labor.

Like any big endeavor there are always others who rally around to help make it possible. I am grateful for the people who have invested their time and energy to bring this book into reality. Certainly I want to thank my wife, Leah, for letting me talk and talk and talk about my ideas. Ailynn Collins for her early editing work. Peggy King for helping me massage it into publishable shape. Jill Cheeks, a coach, for stepping into the wind with a smile and keeping me on track. Thank you to Carolyn Ingermanson for making sure I looked like I took English classes. Thank you to Chad Vivas, a fantastic artist I found through www.fiverr.com, who added color to the book. Finally, to Teri Burns at Lone Mesa Publishing for helping make this book real.

I want to offer a special thanks to Greg McBride. Greg gifted me a life changing opportunity to practice in a beautiful office setting and truly become my potential. He offered support and mentoring without hesitation and taught me to always see the absolute best in others. Thank you all you have done for me.

Perhaps the most important people that have contributed to

this book that I want to truly thank are all my clients over the years. I am grateful for all of you who have come into my office looking to feel better in your relationship and trusting me to offer guidance, ideas and hope. I have always done my absolute best to help repair and heal from the hurts and find ways to connect in that secure and loving way we all crave. I hope too, that all I have learned will show up in this book and give you a chance to find that secure and loving relationship that is, I believe, our life's purpose.

Disclaimer

I would like to be able to write a book that addresses every possible relationship issue and have it become the definitive self-help resource on how to fix a relationship. I would like to tell you that my book is all you will ever need to have a happy, secure, and loving relationship. The more realistic truth is that despite me offering what I hope and believe will be the critical basics that couples must follow, every relationship's history and current dynamic are different. This book is about getting in touch with the basic rules of communication and relationships that as a couple you are probably not doing well or at all.

When big hurts happen and boundaries are crossed, sometimes getting the relationship back on track will require more specific help. This is where counseling may be the right choice. While I believe the steps outlined in my book are the foundational basics of relationships and will help, fully getting back on the rails might require professional help in the form of a counselor.

I write this book as a relationship counselor, a consultant. It is sold with the understanding that the publisher and author are not engaged in rendering legal, accounting, or other professional services. If legal or other expert assistance is required, the services of a competent professional should be sought.

Every effort has been made to make this book to be as complete and as accurate as possible. However, there *may be mistakes*, both typographical and in content. Therefore, this text should be used only as a general guide and not as the ultimate source of relationships and communication information.

The purpose of this book is to educate and entertain. The author and 10 Steps Publishing shall have neither liability nor responsibility to any person or entity with respect to any loss or damage caused, or alleged to have been caused, directly or indirectly, by the information contained in this book.

If you do not wish to be bound by the above, you may return this book to the publisher for a full refund.

If you are the one being "fixed":

First, breathe and count to ten. If you just found this book hidden under a stack of magazines or hiding in your partner's nightstand, *don't panic*. If you're the partner in a relationship that someone is trying to "fix" by buying this book, the first thing you should do is take a breath and chill out because you are not "the problem." In this book I won't be throwing you under the bus or blaming you for all the issues in the relationship. I promise.

Consider reading this book *with* your partner. Engage in conversations about how to better respond to each other and run through the experiments in this book together. If you engage in this process with them, I promise your relationship will feel better. Your partner most likely bought this book to have a better relationship with you. They want to be closer to you and happier with you and to communicate better. For those reasons, I hope you will thank them for purchasing this book. I hope you will join them in making your relationship extra special.

Part 1
Why Relationships Are Messy

Marriage is like riding in a canoe with your partner, floating down the rapids toward a waterfall. To stay clear of danger and survive, both of you need to paddle and steer as a team. If one of you gets mad and whacks the other on the head with the paddle or crosses their arms and refuses to help, you both will go crashing over the falls and drown.

Chapter One

We Can't Communicate!

*Wouldn't it be wonderful if you could take your part-
ner to a "relationship repair facility" and say, "I just
can NOT communicate with my partner. When I try,
they become hugely annoying. Will you fix them,
please? I'm going to do a little shopping and be back
later to pick them up."*

Sure, it all starts out great. You click so perfectly with your
new partner; you question how you made it so far in life
without them. You become best friends who stay up late talking
for hours about each other's deep, dark secrets. The passion is so
intense; it's like your body runs on desire instead of calories.
Heck, you don't even care if you are watching paint dry, just so
long as you're together. Everywhere you look flowers are bloom-
ing and rainbows are glowing, all because you finally found
someone who completely accepts and wants you. Falling in love
is glorious!

Unfortunately life and the proverbial crapola happen. The
real world's demands creep into your dream and dilute the passion. Over time, from lack of nurturing, the flowers wither and

rainbows fade. One day you find yourself feeling alone, wondering what the hell happened. You begin to consider that maybe your partner has an evil twin and that's who you live with sometimes. You know, the evil twin who stomps on flowers and spits on rainbows. Yikes!

Relationships are the foundation that we stand on to face the world. When your relationship is going great, the rest of life's junk isn't so bad. Yet, even when your job is going well and the rest of your life is full, feeling hurt and alone in your relationship will destabilize everything. You lose that sense of I'm going to be okay.

When your relationship isn't working, it's natural to see ways your partner could treat you better and how they could demonstrate that they love you with more convincing oomph. At this point you will probably start to think the thought If only my partner would _____. If they loved me, they would _____. . . If they understood me . . . If they appreciated me . . . If I was important to them . . . They would what? They would treat you better? Love you more? Be more responsive? Maybe they wouldn't criticize you, or be so mean when they are upset? I bet the blanks are easy for you to fill in.

Is this how you feel?

If this is resonating with you so far, let's run through a checklist and see if you ever feel any of the following. Do you feel:

Exhausted? If I were to suggest you go talk about how you feel and what you need in the relationship, would this cause your vital life energy to drain out of your body, leaving only enough to toss this book at me?

19

Unappreciated? Does it seem as though all your efforts to be there for your partner, to do everything they ask, go unacknowledged? Great news! You've become the hired help.

Unimportant? Does your partner always seem to take care of what he or she needs first? When you ask for something small, do you end up feeling disappointed again? You must feel like second or third on their priority list. Or, should I have written twenty-third?

Not Understood? You try to communicate your needs, hoping they will "get it." You talk and talk and talk, yet does it seem as though they have lead shielding in their skull to prevent any of your words or feelings from getting in?

Not Accepted? No matter how hard you work to do everything the "right" way, does your partner still find something wrong? Do you constantly believe that you are not good enough? Did they miss their calling as a white-glove inspector at the local museum of perfection?

Do you feel alone in your relationship?

If you experience any of these things in your relationship, there is a highly technical term to describe what is going on, one that you may identify with: **this sucks!** *Feeling* hurt, unhappy, and maybe even alone in your relationship is the worst. After a while it probably seems as though you are living with a roommate. I bet when you said, "Yes, I will commit to being with you forever," you didn't really mean to say, "Yes, it's okay to ignore me and even if you do I will still do your laundry and clean the toilets, forever."

I can't communicate with my partner!

When individuals or couples come into my office looking for tools to improve their relationship, I ask them what they think is the problem. Usually someone will say, "We do not communicate."

What this really means is *I can't find a way to get my partner to respond to my needs or change in a way that works for me.* These efforts to express needs and wants turn into disagreements and arguments laced with criticism and hurt. Ironically in the midst of fighting to get someone to be more understanding and move closer, partners often say and do things that bring about the absolute opposite.

Couples who are struggling usually fail to repair the hurt and even forget about the issue that started the argument. Instead, the issue is swept under the rug out of sight and the hurt gets stuffed down inside, at least for now. Unfortunately the issue will creep back out when no one is looking, and the hurt will come back up too. Like a bad burrito when you already have food poisoning, it's just not good.

Managing the issues that won't go away takes solid communication between partners. It takes empathy, kindness, agreements, trust, and follow-through. So you are on the right track if you are thinking better communication would help your relationship. However, the real issue is deeper, which is why couples struggle to solve it.

The real issue is responsiveness to each other. Deep in our brain, as I will share in chapter three, no responsiveness equals no relationship, which equals danger. The emotions and reactions that flow from this moment can cause it all to blow up like a match tossed into a pile of gunpowder.

So how do you learn to engage with your partner to get them to respond to your needs and wants? Maybe they started out working just fine, but now seem broken. Can they really be fixed?

Chapter Two

Can I Really "Fix" My Partner?

I wish I could direct you to a website where you could log in to a "customize your partner" account, plug them into a USB port and download a software update right into their brain. We could add things like "always smiles," "says happy things," "never complains," and "listens with empathy and compassion." Adding that they love gourmet cooking and doing laundry might be fun too.

If only this were possible. Unfortunately, you cannot change your partner and neither can I. *Fix Your Partner in 10 Easy Steps or Less!* is not about changing your partner, because that would never work. Rather it is about finding a way to cultivate an emotionally safe and responsive relationship. It is about sending out cues that say, *I care* in order to receive back responses that say, *I care too.*

Fix Your Partner in 10 Easy Steps or Less! is about treating your partner in a manner that motivates them to treat you with love and kindness in return. Yes, I am saying you can train them to treat you better, and that's what we're going to do.

This book is about learning steps to approach and talk to your partner in a way that sends out a clear signal of what you need so they can and will pay attention and actually respond. It also means you will be responding to their needs.

When you communicate with your partner using some of the tools I will lay out, you will be meeting their needs and increase the odds that they will respond in a way that works for you.

Yes, I did just do that. I just suggested that you will have to do some of the work too. I'm sorry, but there is no way around that. You aren't where you want to be in relationship bliss, so something has to change and one of you has to start.

A teacher in my graduate school was fond of saying, "You were elected but didn't run for office."

Someone has to go first, and since you are here reading and they are not, I guess I should say congratulations on your election!

The good news is I am here to help. I am going to make it easy to understand where to work on changing and guide you step by step to try things that are proven to work.

Since communication is at the heart of your relationship's success, we will make sure your words and actions are creating the impact that you intend and have the best chance possible of garnering the response you want.

This brings us to a key fact, one you must learn and live by if you want to make your relationships work.

The big key to relationship success

In order for your relationship to work for you and your partner, you will both have to accept the following basic truth of relationships and make it a way of being. This truth identifies, in one sentence, both the core problem in relationships and the solution at the same time. Ready? It's okay to hold your breath.

Everything is communication with your partner.

It is important to understand and live the belief that no matter what you do, what you say, how you say it, you are always conveying a message. It is important to be aware and mindful of the fact that in almost all interactions, you are either saying, *I care and have your back* or, *I do not care and do not have your back.* This goes for them as well. When you can accept and live by the idea that everything you do or don't do *impacts* your partner, you will increase your chances of success tenfold. Yes, even if you are all by yourself. The shoes you wear, the speed you drive your car, or even where you eat lunch—it all impacts your partner in some way.

Certainly the impact from some decisions or actions is so tiny it might be irrelevant to your partner. If I choose to stop at the grocery store on my way home, it may not matter to my wife. However, if she is home waiting for me, I might want to give her a call so she doesn't wonder or worry where I am. If I do that, I am considering how my decision will impact her. If I show up with only enough chocolate cake for me, I will really be communicating that I don't consider her, and this will hurt her feelings. I may also find myself sleeping alone!

Picture it like this. Each of you has a little black box inside your head through which every decision gets processed before you act on it. This black box takes a potential decision and mixes it with the question "How is this going to impact my partner?"

Today, for example, you'd like to stop off for a drink before heading home from work. Zip! Through the little black box you crank this thought. *How will this impact my partner? What am I about to communicate to them if I take this action?* When you think this way, you will increase the odds of making decisions that help them feel good. This is very important if you want to get them fixed.

You might be thinking, *Wait, this sounds like control!* As we'll learn later, you and your partner have agreed to care for each other. You have agreed to sacrifice some of your freedom in order to enjoy the benefits and security of a relationship. This means you now take on *some* responsibility for the other person. Perhaps un-negotiated, you have also agreed to act in a way that would not upset or hurt the other person irrespective of whether they are present or not. Just because your partner isn't with you doesn't make it okay to have sex with someone else. Unless you have an agreement to the contrary, of course.

My behavior always impacts my wife. If I try to see how fast my car will go up the freeway and she has asked me not to do that, even if she is not in the car, I am still impacting her. I would be using gas and thus money up faster than she might see as reasonable, I could get an expensive ticket, and I might crash and injure myself or someone else, or even die. Since she has asked me not to and I am doing it anyway, I am saying that I will not always be responsive to her requests. All this will impact her, so if I want to convey that she matters to me, if I want her to

26

consider me and my needs, then I have to at least consider her feelings when I make decisions. Just to round this example out, if she finds out and punishes me by yelling and screaming, calling me names, or ignoring me for a week, then we *are* moving into the control column. That's a problem we'll cover in a bit.

Will they really change if I change?

You're probably wondering if your partner will really change if you follow the steps in this book. Healthy skepticism is good! So let's consider the concept of change for a moment, because understanding this will help you build confidence in the steps I will outline later.

In terms of human behavior, and based on the study of how systems change, there are two reasons why a system, or person, will change:

1. Because the pressure and tension is so great, they must change to survive.
2. Because they see something on the horizon they want.

If you've ever tried to get your partner to respond to you (and change) through what you think is witty sarcasm, sneaky verbal jabs, by yelling loudly to make sure they hear you or even by throwing something to get their attention, you have already tried the pressure-and-tension approach. Be honest now—most of us have tried this method at one time or another. How well have you seen it work?

One time a couple came in after having a few weeks of fights. He complained that when his wife became angry she would break something of his. When I asked her about this, she rolled her eyes and said, "Of course! That's the only way I can get

27

him to listen to me." Sure, that's one way, though a bit expensive no doubt. It won't work in the long run because of how it hurts her husband. I hope you'll be game to try an easier and more pleasant way, the second method. Let's go for building good feelings in your partner.

Later, as you go through the ten steps in this book, you will learn tools for expressing your needs and responding to your partner in a way that will up the odds for a response that is helpful. You'll also see how to give out samples of a secure and loving relationship, and that will feel good. We are designed to be in a relationship because it is safer; it improves our chances for survival in this big, bad world. At least, the goal is for it to feel that way.

Good news: perfection is not necessary

When you are miserable in a relationship and working toward improvement, it can seem like the entire world will have to change, mountains will have to move, before you can possibly feel better. The amount of blood, sweat, and tears it will take to fix things seems overwhelming.

However, the truth and good news is that many times just a little ten percent adjustment can make a big difference. Think about this: if you could get ten percent more kindness, ten percent more connection, ten percent more responsiveness, or ten percent more affection, would you feel some relief? Would you see more hope? What if you see another ten percent improvement the next week or even the next month? I realize that you can't quantify things this way, and yet if you could get an incremental change that helps you feel better; it's possible that by next week, you could make another small change to feel even better! In this way your relationship can be trending upwards toward "extra special" instead of hovering around "just good enough" or, worse, trending down toward "get me out of here!"

What if it doesn't work?

Of course I cannot guarantee that if you change your approach, your partner will change their response. There are too many variables for me to make a guarantee. For instance, if your partner abuses alcohol or drugs, or is having an affair, the ability to get your partner to respond is impeded. This makes rebuilding the relationship difficult. In which case, there might be more work to do beyond the scope of this book. A professional counselor might be a good choice to consider.

However, if you follow the steps in this book, I am confident in saying things will at least be somewhat better even if your partner still doesn't engage or respond in a way that works for you. If this is the case, at least *you* will be putting in a sincere effort to clean up your contribution and improve your communication. This may help you feel better if your partner tries to sell the idea that you are the problem. You will also be gathering important information about what improvement is possible, and what is not. This all brings up a difficult yet predictable question, and one you have probably been pondering late at night when you can't sleep.

Is my partner worth fixing?

Yup, I can hear you thinking this. *Is my relationship worth working on?* Honestly, I don't blame you for asking. When you get into a place where it seems every moment with your partner is a painful struggle; when gears grind and tears flow, how could you not ask that question?

Since it is not my place to pass judgment on anyone's relationship, I will answer your question in typical therapist fashion, with three questions for you in return. Consider these, and you may have your answer. Or, you will realize you need to gather more information to determine your answer to this important question.

1. Do you believe your partner is capable of meeting your needs?

If deep down you do not believe that they are actually physically, humanly capable, then that is a problem. You can't get a fish to go on a hike. This means you might be facing the challenge of accepting "what is" and working to decide if you want to continue accepting it or not.

Is your partner physically and emotionally capable of sharing their feelings? Can they be compassionate? Are they physically and/or emotionally able to be there for you when you need and request help?

We all bring deficits to a relationship, and sometimes one person's deficit is too much for the other to accept. If you need more emotional responsiveness and your partner has Asperger's, you may struggle to realign your expectations. If your partner is forgetful and wrestles with Attention Deficit Disorder, for example, you may have to accept this to be in the relationship.

These types of realities can change the way someone responds, not because they do not care, but because it's how they are physically wired. You will have to decide if you can accept the reality or not. Usually we do believe our partners are physically capable. So the problem is not one of capability but rather one of willingness.

2. Do you believe your partner is willing to work on meeting your needs?

Assuming you got past question number one, ask yourself if your partner is willing to invest the time and effort to learn how to meet your needs. Are they willing to make sacrifices to be with you? Are they willing to try to meet your needs to improve the relationship?

Putting the debate about reincarnation aside for a moment, I'll suggest that you only get one go-around. I have this view that our purpose in life is to love and be loved, so if you are with someone who is unwilling to care for you and try to meet your relationship needs, assuming you are meeting theirs, is it worth your time here on our big, beautiful planet? Again, working on these steps to gather more information to confirm this belief before you make big decisions may help you feel better about whatever decision you might make.

3. Am I willing to work toward meeting my partner's needs?

If you are feeling unhappy, alone, disconnected, unimportant, or unappreciated, this is most likely because you believe your partner is not meeting your needs. At the same time I can just about guarantee that your partner is running around the chicken coop believing that you do not meet their needs either, hence the deadlock.

They may even be reading this book too, hoping I can fix you!

This is always the ironic part: people often want the same things and feel the same thing is missing in the relationship. I always joke that if partners followed the Golden Rule of treating others like you want to be treated, I wouldn't have a job! This is easy to understand, but hard to follow.

What if you are completely burned out on giving? So much so that the very thought of my suggestion of you going first to try and meet your partner's needs makes you want to use this book as a doorstop?

I completely acknowledge that you might be feeling this way. If you have been struggling and fighting to get your partner to respond, but he or she has come up short, of course you are going to feel distraught. I realize you may not be open to trying again, *but someone has to go first*. If it is going to be you, let's first make sure you are set up to be successful.

Time to dig in

This book is structured so that you will be able to gain insight into various potential problems and have lots of experiments to try, step by step. While it is best if both partners are working together at the same time with collaboration and the intention to meet each other's needs, one person can still change how the relationship feels to be in. Yes, one person can get a relationship moving toward the "good enough" category. Ready?

Assuming you made it through those three questions and are still here with me, it must mean you believe *or at least want to believe* your partner is capable and willing. Fantastic! Let's get started.

Chapter Three

Why We Attach

Assuming your partner is human—feel free to double-check, I'll wait. Yes? Great! As much as they are a unique individual, they are also a member of the human race. This means their behavior is highly predictable.

If you want to break out of the negative communication cycle in your relationship, you have to understand what it looks like and how each of you contributes. You can skip ahead to the steps starting in chapter six, but please don't. These next three chapters are going to set you up to be an expert on your partner and your relationship. If you are going to fix your partner, you need to know what makes them tick.

Let's start with why humans are driven to be in relationships in the first place. As you'll see, it isn't just to have someone around to do your laundry or mow the lawn. It's about getting your needs met, not just your wants. One of the biggest needs that all humans have from the cradle to the grave is the need to be connected to others. It is my personal and professional belief that this is because humans are not designed to be alone.

Deep in the part of our brain that is focused on making sure we survive is the belief that being alone is dangerous. It has been that way for literally 100,000 or so years. If humans were designed to be alone, a cave baby would have popped out, grabbed a spear, and headed off into the jungle on its own. Your children would be driven to do the same; to separate from you earlier in life. Instead, a human baby's survival is completely and totally dependent on another, so they stay around *for years.*

To help protect you from when you are born and through your lifetime, nature gave you an emotional system as standard equipment. This way if you experience a threat, say someone standing over you with a two-by-four aimed at your head, you will react, driven by fear, to protect yourself. Without emotion, you might not react to a danger in time to be safe. In this case your body's fight-or-flight system will activate, the chemicals of fear will flood your body and get you to do something to survive. Duck! Fight! Run!

That example makes sense because the two-by-four was a physical threat, but what if the danger is not physical? Let's say you come home from work one day, and find your partner has packed their bags and is loading them into the car. There isn't a threat to your physical safety in that moment, yet you probably wouldn't utter a "hi" and go calmly make yourself a peanut-butter-and-pickle sandwich. The belief that your partner is leaving would be highly emotional and thus motivate you do to something about the perceived threat. If you believe your partner is rejecting or abandoning you, isn't that threatening to your sense of security in the world? If you truly care about the relationship, this would probably *feel* as though a two-by-four was aimed at your head and your stomach too.

Your brain monitors communication

Your brain is pretty smart. Its number one priority is to make sure you survive. As such, it is constantly on alert monitoring your environment for threats to the safety and security of your relationships. Long ago human brains learned that when their humans stay together in a group, the odds of survival go way up. Being around others that will support, nurture, and protect is a good thing. Our brains learned:

Relationship = Survival

This monitoring system in your body is called the **attachment** system. The system works to make sure you stay connected, or attached, to those around you who seem most likely to help if you are in need. Your brain's contribution to the attachment system is to monitor all communication and analyze it for signs of threat to the relationship.

Behind the scene, between the lines, and in every situation all the time, your brain is asking the following types of questions. We'll call these the *attachment monitoring* questions. These are questions such as:

- o Do I matter?
- o Can I trust this person?
- o Does this person want me?
- o Does this person care if I am hurt?
- o Will this person respond to me if I need them?

If the answers come back as "Yes," then the green light stays on and life rolls along like fluffy pancakes covered in maple syrup: smooth and yummy. If any answers come back as "Maybe," a yellow warning light gets switched on and your brain will become alert and vigilant. Now life is more like a white-knuckle drive on a winding road along a cliff. Your brain will begin anxiously monitoring everything that is communicated. *What is the intention of this person? Where is the threat? There must be a threat here; I can't risk not finding it!* Because thoughts create feelings, these thoughts lead to anxious feelings.

If the answers to those attachment monitoring questions start coming back as "No," then red lights in your head will flash danger! "No" answers tell the attachment system there is a clear and present threat to the relationship and therefore your survival. When threatened, aircraft carriers launch fighter jets loaded with missiles and bombs. The human brain (thankfully) doesn't have missiles and bombs. Instead it has an emotional system.

Over our lifetime the experiences we have help us create meaning from what happens around us. This helps us quickly and easily read a situation to create meaning from what is communicated to us. If I am talking and my wife interrupts me, I will conclude that she is not listening, because I've had that same experience in my past. My brain then makes meaning. It determines that if my wife is not listening, she is probably not interested in what I am eager to share. Then it can get worse.

In that moment I instinctively believe that my need is less important to her and therefore by my attachment system's calculation, *I am less important.* Red alert! My brain will activate my emotional system to get me feeling a certain way. In this case, my feelings will hurt. This is my attachment system's way of getting me to do something about this threat.

Six attachment needs

There are six needs that your brain uses to categorize all communication and keep track of your safety and security in a relationship. These help your brain determine whether *I am loved and safe* or *I am not loved and not safe*. Knowing these about yourself and your partner will help you build a road map to a better connection.

To feel safe and secure, humans all NEED to be:

1. *Appreciated* for our efforts
2. *Accepted* as we are
3. *Important* to the other
4. *Understood* at a deep level
5. *Close*, which equals security
6. And have the people we are close to reflect the good in us. We want them to believe we are a good person, believe we have good intentions, and say nice things about us when we are not around. We don't want the other person to write evil stories in their head about us and our intentions.

When you are in a relationship with someone, you will want these needs to be met. If they are not, the relationship will feel less secure. The more of these you do not get met in the relationship, the more emotionally painful the relationship will be. Of course, when you do not meet these needs for your partner, they will not be feeling close to you either. This makes it imperative for you each to know the other's key needs. Meeting their needs helps them feel valuable and motivates them to meet your needs in return.

Get in touch with your own attachment needs

Let's see if we can flush out your own key attachment needs and perhaps tune you in to your partner's with a quick and easy exercise. Repeat each statement below a few times, and let each one soak in before moving to the next. Allow yourself a moment to let any associated thoughts and feelings inside your body grow.

Fill in the blank with your partner's name. See if you can feel which one or two are bigger.

I am not important to _____.

I am not appreciated by _____.

_____ does not accept me.

_____ does not understand me.

_____ does not think I am a good person.

I do not feel close to _____.

Do any of these create stronger feelings inside you than the others? You and your partner and every human need them all; however, oftentimes one or two feel bigger than the others. When your partner somehow communicates that you are NOT appreciated, accepted, understood, important, or close, or that they do not believe you are a good person, you will get emotional.

Emotions are signals that you have a need. Naturally, you want a partner who will pay attention to that emotional signal and respond in a way that helps you feel better. Emotions are pretty important. We'll cover them next.

Chapter Takeaway:

We all want to be appreciated, accepted, important, understood, close and have those close to us reflect we are a good person. Having those needs doesn't make you "needy" it makes you human.

Chapter Four

Why We Have Emotions

Say you're out walking in the woods and suddenly a bear jumps out of the bushes. If you didn't have emotions, this would be an intellectual moment of observation and curiosity. You might think, Hmm, he looks fuzzy. I wonder if he's hungry?

The truth is that we have not descended from any early humans who were without emotions. Any who may have existed were eaten. You need emotions to survive. In the case of the bear, without a surge of chemicals to create the feelings of fear, you may not be compelled to act in some way to protect yourself and survive. The bear isn't going to see you're scared and meet your attachment needs with a warm and fuzzy bear hug, and your brain knows this. He's just going to eat you, and that's scary! Run! Or actually, I think you're supposed to play dead. Good luck!

I've been suggesting that when your brain sees a threat to your relationship, it launches your emotional system. Emotions are the part of this system that gets you to move. In fact, the word *emotion* comes from a Latin word, *ēmovēre*, which means "to move." Emotions exist in order to move you into action. They create the urge to get off your duff and do something, often about a perceived threat.

Thankfully (or hopefully), you're not in a relationship with a bear. Most likely your partner is another human. This is good because it means they are predictable. Predictability means you have a chance to anticipate and respond to each other's emotions and underlying needs. Doing so strengthens the trust and security between you. If you or your partner is not good at recognizing and responding to the other in a comforting way, the relationship will be emotionally painful.

Emotions signal you have a need

I believe that emotions are so connected to those attachment needs that I am willing to go out on a theoretical ledge and suggest that:

All emotions are related to an attachment need.

By this I mean that anytime you have an emotion, there is a natural longing inside of you for another person, someone you trust, to be there and respond. No matter what, you want someone to understand you, and be there. Theoretical debate aside, I am willing to bet you will agree with me that in life, the more emotional moments you experience tend to surround relationships. Anytime you are criticized, dismissed, or ignored by someone that matters to you, your brain will generate an emotion. That emotion comes with a specific urge to do something to get the relationship back to a safe state of being.

41

How your brain calculates which emotion to use

Let us say that you are going about your day with the blue-bird of happiness whistling on your shoulder. Hooray! Then something happens. Maybe that bluebird poops on your head before flying away. Life is not so good. When your five senses are exposed to an experience, they send information to your brain for processing. Your brain quickly runs a complicated algorithm to figure out how t o respond to the event. Remember, it always prioritizes your survival. Your brain calculates:

- o   Your current needs for safety and security
- o   Your beliefs and memories of past experiences
- o   The possible future consequences of this moment

This all happens instantaneously because your brain's thoughts and body's emotions must be quick enough to save your life. It then decides which emotion is most likely going to get you moving to help you get back to a safe, secure, and happy place.

Four primary emotions

There are three primary colors, red, yellow, and blue. Every other color is a combination of these. Emotions are the same way, except there are four. An easy way to remember the four primary emotions is through a not-so-good rhyme: mad, sad, glad, and scared. Not perfect, but it works. Every other emotion is either a degree or a combination of these four. Things like frustrated, annoyed, bummed, and worried are degrees of sadness, anger, or fear. Emotions such as shame, guilt, or hurt are combinations of the four basic emotions. Let's get out our crayons and run through them.

Glad = Happiness = More!

Human beings want to be happy. Happiness is the state of being we work to create. We engage in hobbies, build close relationships, and find jobs that fulfill us. We are particular about where we live, the car we drive, and the clothing we wear. We choose colors, shapes, etc., all because we want to feel a sense of happiness. That Einstein guy had it right when he said that everything is relative. The state of happiness is the ruler we use to measure what we are feeling. We ask ourselves, *Will this lead to more happiness or not?*

When we express happiness, our face looks light and bright. We smile, our body language is open and bubbly, and there is a pleasant energy around us that communicates to others that we are indeed happy. We make decisions in life that we believe will lead to being happy. And when we're happy, isn't it always better having someone with us to share it?

Scared = Danger = Need to Be Safe

Let's say that after running all the computations, your brain determines that fear is the appropriate emotion that will bring about your best chance of survival. Your body will be flooded with little neuropeptides that attach to certain key cells and create the feeling of an emotion—in this case the uncomfortable feeling of fear. Now you want relief from this icky feeling and want to feel safe again. You will then be motivated to act in some way that will bring about relief from the feelings fear brings.

You might express your fear through a facial expression of fright, posturing to fight, running, or cowering in a little ball on the ground. Either way, the main urge is to be safe so you can get back to feeling calm and happy. Fear motivates you to do something about your safety. Fear motivates you to protect yourself. "Help me, I'm scared!" Yes, another person can often help us feel better when we're scared.

Sad = Alone = Need Connection

Maybe you are having a good day when you get a phone call with news that someone important to you has packed up and moved to Bali to teach yoga. Your body runs the emotional algorithm and determines that you probably are never going to see them again, and you are sad. Your brain then signals your body to release the chemicals of sadness. This creates an uncomfortable feeling that you know will be eased if you can just feel close to someone.

You long for the person that is gone and know you cannot reach for them. In that moment tears may flow as a signal of your emotion. You want someone to hold you, tell you it will be okay and won't last forever.

If and when you can get some of that need for connection met, you might not be happy right away, of course, but your emotion is on its way to being soothed.

Mad = Unfair and Powerless = Need Change

This leaves mad as the last primary emotion. When you are mad, it will be because something feels unfair and is often woven together with a sense of powerlessness. If you believe someone is treating you unfairly, such as taking cuts in line or not letting you switch lanes on the freeway, you will feel mad. If someone accuses you of eating the last chocolate bar when you didn't, you will probably get angry.

The emotion of mad or anger is a bit more complex than

scared or sad because sometimes people are rightly mad and other times they are just being reactive. Yelling, cursing, and name-calling are examples of reactions. We'll talk about reactions in the next chapter. For now let's deal with the primary emotion of being mad.

The true emotion of anger is an important one because it motivates you to do something about the injustice, to stand up for yourself or another and push for justice and fairness. Feeling powerless can also lead to being mad because if you are powerless, you are not free to make choices that lead to happiness. If you are not free, something is most definitely unfair, which motivates you to fight for your freedom and boundaries. You fight to be treated a certain way, which is fairly.

In your body, anger may come with a rush of adrenaline and a raised heart rate. You might express this by getting a scowling face, posturing for battle, and becoming tense, readying yourself to defend your boundaries. This desire to stand up for yourself, your freedom, and your boundaries is the urge that the emotion of being mad creates. When you are angry and can feel heard or validated, when you can change the situation, perhaps by renegotiating with the person you are angry at, you will feel better.

Imagine if you weren't in touch with your emotions. Maybe you know someone like that, like maybe your partner? If you or your partner is not aware of the feelings inside, then you cannot recognize the impulse within that emotion. You lose a huge internal compass designed to help you navigate life and relationships. It gets worse, though. It's one thing to work on identifying feeling sad or scared or mad, but what if you are feeling two or more emotions at once?

While mixing two or more colors creates a new color, sometimes a pretty one and sometimes not, mixing emotions often creates a mess. Let's sort out a couple important emotions that crop up a lot in relationships, emotions that are a messy mixture of these primary ones.

Hurt = Mad + Sad + Scared

Hurt is a combination of being mad, sad, and scared all at once. The problem that occurs when you feel three emotions at once is that you are being urged in three different directions at the same time. This can create a sense of being overwhelmed or flooded. It can paralyze you from taking action because you're not sure which need to focus on first for the best outcome.

Let's say one of the most painful relationship things happen; you learn your partner had an affair. The hurt will be a messy combination of emotions.

Anger wants you to stand up for yourself and protest the unfairness. It wants you to set a boundary and protect yourself from being hurt again. Sadness wants you to draw them closer so you can receive comfort from the hurt and feel protected. Fear may motivate you to push them away because they are the source of your pain and could hurt you again. You won't trust them right now out of self-preservation.

This messy combination of emotions pulling you in conflicting directions can leave you stuck. How do you cope with hurt? Which emotion do you prioritize? Do you risk asking your partner, the person who hurt you, for help? Do you react with anger and attack with criticism? Do you shut down and refuse to talk to your partner?

These questions are hard to answer in the midst of feeling pain and make up the difficulty of dealing with the huge hurts that can happen in relationships. This is why sometimes deep hurts become so paralyzing that couples seek counseling for help to sort through this jungle and find a path to repair.

Shame = Sad + Fear + Low Self-esteem

When you mix low self-esteem with not getting your basic needs for connection met, shame is the painful result. It creates the belief that you may not be a lovable or a good person.

This seed may have been planted when you were little or later while you were in a difficult relationship. Either way, it feels like a deep, dark, painful place is inside that you avoid at all costs. The sense you might have is that if you go there, there is no way out.

Shame includes a mixture of sadness and fear. The sadness is a cue that you need someone else to move close, to accept and comfort you. However, since that would be vulnerable and therefore risky, fear compels you to shy away from others. You can't risk moving closer because deep down you hold the fear that you may not be worthy. If you did risk opening up and they were to truly "see" you as you see yourself, unlovable, there is no way they would accept you. Being alone seems like the only option. See how it feels all thick and sticky? Like being tarred and feathered. Yuck!

A tiny sense of inner shame can be a good thing. It motivates you to be diligent about your relationship and look after is by working to be valuable. However, too much shame (and low self-esteem) will prevent you from fully engaging in the expression of your needs. This keeps you separate and can prevent your partner from knowing how to meet your needs. It also keeps them feeling left out which can feed into their own sense of unworthiness. Not a good spiral to be in.

Guilt = Mad + Sad + Scared + Regret + Shame

This brings us to guilt. Guilt is complex, but important for us to unpack because it is part of relationships. Honestly I could write another whole book, just on guilt! It has a good, even helpful side, but a deep, dark side too.

Guilt is a combination of sadness, fear, and anger with a dose of regret and a pinch of shame tossed in. As an emotion itself, guilt compels you to confront yourself and change how you act or make decisions. Guilt is an internal dialogue that goes like:

1. *I am mad at myself for making this decision. I should have* _____. *I shouldn't have* _____.
2. *I am sad and want to be forgiven, and scared I may not be.*
3. *I will never do that again because I am ashamed of myself and never want to feel this way ever again!*

The goal is to work through these thoughts and get to number three. If you can commit to a change and stop judging yourself as unworthy, you will find your way out of the guilt cycle.

Guilt is part of the delicate balance that creates responsiveness in relationships. I want my wife to be happy, so I am motivated to respond to her needs and wants. I don't want to feel bad about her feeling bad. If she asks me to pick her up some milk on the way home from work and I forget, her disappointment will impact me and I will be upset at myself; I will feel guilty for letting her down. That motivation to respond comes from my own desire to avoid feeling badly about myself and to avoid doing anything to contribute to her feeling disappointed in me.

This can go badly too. Because guilt contains a sense of inner shame, it can be used in manipulative ways. Sometimes people learn to communicate their own needs through guilt, such as "If

you loved me, you would have stopped by the store for me."
Statements like these try to connect your need for acceptance
and love, with your fear of being unworthy of love or the fear of
not being a good person (shame), with their need or want. This
approach is manipulative, sort of an emotional blackmail. Meeting someone's needs out of guilt won't build a happy relationship,
because instead of feeling joyful to give to your partner, you will
hurt and become resentful.

Wow, we've covered quite a lot about human behavior in
these last two chapters! We talked about how humans need relationships and how when our brain perceives a threat to our close
relationships, we get emotional. In this chapter we got through
the primary emotions along with the combinations of hurt,
shame, and guilt. If this is starting to sound a bit overwhelming,
don't panic! I have not been covering what to do about all this
stuff because that is in the steps. In fact, you will see that by following the steps, working on this stuff is easy, just like eating
pancakes. Now it is time for us to cover the last piece of human
behavior in relationships so you can see how the negative cycle of
relationships goes wild. As you will see in the next chapter, our
reactions to emotions are *THE BIG PROBLEM* in relationships,
not the emotions themselves.

Chapter Takeaway:

Attachment needs activate your emotions. If you do not feel appreciated, accepted, important, close, understood or reflected in a
good way, you will have an emotion. The emotion is a signal you
have a need. Identify what you are feeling and you have a better
chance of figuring out what you need to feel better again.

Happy   = Give me more! Come share with me.

Mad   = This is unfair; I am powerless = I need change.

Sad   = I feel alone = I need to feel connection.

Scared   = I do not feel safe = I need to feel safe again.

Chapter Five

Reactivity Will Wreck Your Relationship

You finally get the car of your dreams. Congrats! Yet, what if every time you get mad about something, you cope with your feelings by going out and beating it with a hammer? Eventually that dream car will be a pile of junk no one wants, not even you.

I've been sharing my perspective on human behavior, because if you understand it, your partner becomes more predictable. When you understand your partner enough to anticipate their behavior and responses, you can better choose how to evoke a response you want and avoid what you don't want. That's how we're going to fix them. Remember, we're not talking about manipulation or control. We are talking about approaching your partner in a way that has a good chance of evoking a helpful response from them, so you can get your needs met. Ironically they will too.

We've covered the key attachment needs all humans have and how emotions are activated when one or more of those needs aren't met. Now let's wrap up this section on human behavior. To do that we need just one more piece of the puzzle, so you will have a clear understanding of why your relationship hurts sometimes. Let's begin with an example.

Maybe late one night you can't sleep and decide to pass the hours by baking cookies, naturally, from scratch. Instead of using a manual stirring system—a spoon—to mix the batter, you get out the 800 horsepower turbo mixer. Yes, the one with the triple-loud exhaust. When this wakes up your partner, what happens when they come downstairs? You can imagine they might be upset. In the last chapter, we learned that when something feels unfair, when you or your partner doesn't feel important, emotions will follow. That part makes sense. However, this doesn't mean they have the freedom to treat you any way they want just because their feelings are hurt. But that's exactly what partners do to each other, sometimes in very hurtful ways.

"WHAT THE HELL ARE YOU DOING?! YOU'RE SUCH AN IDIOT! WHAT'S WRONG WITH YOU?" If that's what happens when they come down the stairs, your partner is *reacting* to their emotions. This reaction is laden with contempt and criticism, so it is an attack that hurts. Your partner wants you to comply. They want relief from their own crummy feeling of not being considered in your decision to use the turbo mixer. Yet, when they approach you by yelling and being critical, are you drawn to comply and help them feel better? Or do you hit the turbo boost in defiance and yell back, "WHAT? I CAN'T HEAR YOU!"

Reactions are like a slap

The problem with reactive behavior in a relationship is that it often feels like an emotional slap in the face. Slapping your partner will never get them to respond well. When you feel attacked, belittled, criticized, when your partner curses at you or calls you a vulgar name, do you feel like complying? I doubt it. Those are contemptuous reactions that wreck the emotional safety in the relationship. They tear at the security between partners and will eventually break the attachment bond.

So no, you cannot physically or emotionally slap the other person and then say, "You should be able to take my anger. I'm just venting." That's like saying, "I'm just going to slap you sometimes when I get really angry or hurt. You should be able to take it and be okay." No, that's never going to happen. You can't do it to your car and expect it to stay nice. You can't do it to your partner and be happy in the relationship, and they cannot do it to you.

We'll talk about what to do with reactive behavior in the ten steps. Right now my goal is for you to understand and recognize what reactive behavior looks like. Thankfully there are really only two types of responses for us to categorize: reactive anger and withdrawal.

Reactive anger

Despite using the same word, reactive *anger* is not the emotion of being angry or mad. Reactive anger is what someone does in response to an emotion. To be clear, this is what you or your partner CHOOSES to do with the emotion. No matter if you or they think it was chosen or not, everyone is responsible for their own behavior. You can't blame it on someone else.

If I am disappointed that my wife didn't buy me a Ferrari for my birthday, that's my emotion and one I am entitled to have. If in my disappointment I yell, "You're always such a beeyatch!" and slam the door, those are *my* reactions to *my* emotions. No one *made* me say or do those things. At some point, irrespective of what anyone else might do, as an adult I will have to own my own behavior.

I will have to own my reaction, apologize for calling her a mean name and promise not to ever do it again (and follow through!) That is, if I want to keep the relationship emotionally safe.

The primary emotion underneath reactive anger can certainly be angry or mad (something feels unfair); however, it could also be sad, scared, hurt, or something other than angry. We call it *reactive anger* because what we see someone do in response to their emotions *looks* like anger.

Reactive anger includes behavior such as:

o   Raising your voice
o   Name-calling
o   Criticizing
o   Attacking
o   Blaming
o   Bullying
o   Eye rolling
o   Shaking your head
o   Slamming a door
o   Cursing
o   Throwing or breaking something
o   Pointing at your partner
o   Mumbling something under your breath
o   Guffawing—the release of breath that communicates disgust
o   And of course, yelling. "Yelling" can be raising your voice, but also being intense.

Basically, when you or your partner has a hurt feeling (a combination of feeling mad, sad, and scared) and then goes on the attack in some way, it is a reaction. Their reaction will hurt you because it will usually look like criticism, sarcastic comments, defensiveness (blaming), or somehow communicates disgust. All these things hurt, so it is understandable that you may become defensive, shut-down, attack back, even though you don't have to. It's like you're possessed and playing a role you didn't sign up to play.

Reactivity can be big or small; obviously the bigger it is the worse things get. If you're in the car and tell your partner to take a left when it should be a right, they might get a little frustrated. There's the emotion. As a reaction perhaps they roll their eyes, which is contempt. It's like saying, *You're such an idiot.* Maybe they jab you with "Why can't you read a map?" That's hurtful criticism. You might call them out and say, "Hey that hurts." Yet, what if they get defensive and blame you? "Well, it's your fault we're going to be late." That will just add fuel to the fire and make things worse. If one of you can just say, "Hey, I'm sorry I got so frustrated at you", things would feel better fast.

Ironically, the reactive anger you or your partner might be expressing could actually be a protest. If they are feeling unimportant or disconnected, your partner might verbally jab and poke at you. Or, do you do the same to them? Maybe you feel scared because you believe you don't matter to them, so you make a sarcastic comment to draw attention to your hurt. This makes sense because you are trying to get them to respond to the emotional distress you feel. When you prick your partner and they snap back, your attachment system gets an emotion out of them. It's like a dose of good news: *You matter!* Yet, you still won't feel good if they react in return.

55

At the root of reactive anger, there is still a perceived unmet need and a resulting emotion that craves attention. The reactivity is just a way of coping with the emotions of the moment. Reactive anger is bigger, louder, scary, and often seen as the problem in a relationship. That's debatable because feeling abandoned is pretty bad too.

Reactionary distance and withdrawal

Reactionary distance or withdrawal is the other side of the same coin. When your partner feels hurt in some way, do they shut down? If your partner copes with their emotions in this way, perhaps they put on a blank face and stop sharing. Maybe they become defensive or placating. They could even physically leave the room or emotionally withdraw, *sometimes for days*. No matter, when one of you withdraws and is no longer truly engaged in the situation, the other will feel hurt.

Remember, reactions don't get anyone's needs met because of how they impact the other person. If your partner shuts down, you will probably feel dropped, rejected, or even abandoned. As a result you might go on the attack or withdraw yourself. These are all reactions that will continue to pull another reaction from the other and fuel more of the same. They are also connected to painful feelings that don't draw you towards them. Instead, their reaction, their distancing, puts you in emotional distress and repels you.

Becoming distant may seem to bring less negative energy to the moment, but truthfully the resulting hurt or even damage is problematic for the relationship. If you shut down, you are not responsive to your partner and to their attachment system. This signals to them that they *do not matter; there is no relationship*. Those red lights start flashing in their head! If in response, they react by snapping with reactionary anger or by shutting down themselves, it fuels the negative dance between you and prevents repair. Now you are both hurt, upset, angry, and disconnected.

At the root of shutting down, there is still a perceived unmet need and basic emotional hurt. The reactivity is a way of coping with the emotional pain. Often, it is not seen as damaging as the reactive anger side; however, it is, because of how it impacts the other person. To understand what to do about this, let's look at where this reactivity begins.

The parent vs. the child brain

Does all this reactive behavior remind you of a two-year-old having a tantrum? It should, because in a way there is a two-year-old inside your brain. Visualize your brain as having two parts. There are more, of course, but let's keep it simple and focus on just two. You have a "thinking and reasoning" brain, which we'll call your parent brain. Then there is your "fight-or-flight" brain, which we'll call your child brain. By "child" I mean like a two-year-old child. You've heard of the terrible twos? Yes, your brain has one of those inside. Where it comes from will help you see why psychotherapists always want to talk about your childhood.

During a child's first twelve months, life is all about needs. Since they are completely dependent on the adults in their life, pretty much everything that a child gets emotional about is truly a need. They need to eat, sleep and get their diaper changed. When the adults meet these needs with some comforting arms and a warm voice, they feel safe and secure. *Life is good!*

When that child gets to be about twelve months old, things start to change. In addition to all the same needs, they start having wants too. The problem is that when they express that want, it will look the same as a need, since that's the only strategy they know. Besides, it's always worked before. The child will have a tantrum and scream if you don't feed them, and they will do the same if you don't give them the shiny red mug of hot coffee on the table. When these wants start cropping up, parents have two very important responsibilities to prepare that child for managing the rest of their life.

First, a parent must help that child learn to express their needs and wants in an effective way. Children who learn that having a tantrum or being bossy is how to get their way become teens and adults who learn to manipulate others. Maybe you know someone like that? They aren't fun people to be around.

The second thing that parents must do is help the child learn is to regulate their emotions. By this I mean they must help that child's parent brain grow and become strong because eventually it must take their place. This means the parent has to help the child's parent brain learn to curb the impulses and urges that emotions bring. Not hitting Bobby when he takes your favorite fire truck and using calm words to solve the problem is an important life lesson. So is learning to deal with the emotions of frustration and disappointment when somehow the fire truck gets broken and is gone forever. In the same way, your parent brain has to help calm your child brain when hurt feelings occur after your partner has come home late without calling. When disappointed, hurt, sad, scared, or mad, how do you or your partner handle those emotions? Does your parent brain help manage things, or does the child brain take over and have a little tantrum? I'm not being sarcastic here. When your child brain takes control and has a little tantrum, this is its way of coping with the hurt feelings and trying to get someone to respond.

58

Any response is better than no response

Since your relationship is very important to your safety and security, your ability to draw your partner toward you for help is critical. It is a marker of the health of the attachment bond between you. If your partner does not care that you are hurting and will not respond, this could mean you are alone. Your brain sees that as a threat to your survival.

To your brain, especially your child brain, when you express a need and resulting emotion, *any response is better than no response.* If you do not impact your partner emotionally, if they will not respond to you, there is no relationship. To deal with a lack of response, your child brain will start ramping things up. There is a primal panic that happens, and coping reactions fill the room. The insane aspect of this is that oftentimes both partners will do more of what already is *not* working! They yell louder, criticize more, or ignore the other even longer. Of course, this predictably draws the *opposite* of the response that is wanted.

Reactions are self-defeating

Here is the nutty part. When you express yourself through a coping reaction, instead of a soothing, reassuring response, you pull from your partner more of what fuels your own hurt. Again, this happens because of how reactions impact the other person. However insane, when any of us can't manage our own hurt feelings, we make choices that make our own hurt feelings worse.

If I am hurt that my wife hasn't included me in her plans for the day and I react to my hurt by criticizing her, "You are always planning things without me. You never include me."

I will have just hurt her feelings in retaliation. I've stuck a

59

knife into her deep fear that perhaps I think she always has evil intentions (that I don't reflect the good in her). In response to her hurt she will probably say, "Well, *now* I'm not going to spend time with you. I don't want to risk being criticized all day!" She moves away from me, the person who hurt her.

Both reactionary anger and withdrawal remove the emotional safety and security from the relationship. Both responses communicate, "I don't have your back right now, and in fact, I will punish or drop you if you get out of line." In this situation, how can you be vulnerable with your needs and feelings? How can you be intimate?

If you are on the receiving end of a partner who expresses their emotions through reactionary anger or shut down, you will learn to avoid anything that might upset them. This includes risking being close both physically and emotionally.

You will learn not to tell them everything. You will learn to hide things. You will learn not to ask them for help. Life will be about walking on eggshells to avoid your partner's reactions. The problem is that your avoidance will make it worse for them and their short fuse might grow shorter.

Ironically, your partner often really wants you to be more attentive and more helpful, to initiate sex, and to talk to them more, and that's why they are upset all the time. However, you won't move toward them because you might do it wrong and get punished. The risk is too great.

Reactionary anger and withdrawal remove the emotional safety from the relationship. Apologies only work if the hurt stops. Oftentimes reactionary anger or withdrawal becomes default behavior that neither partner trusts can ever change. So, you become stuck in a painful relationship.

No excuses

In a conversation to repair a hurtful situation that includes this reactive behavior we're talking about, you might hear someone say, "I was just angry, and you should be okay with it." Or, "I'm just venting." You might also hear, "I was ignoring you because I didn't want to keep fighting." These are excuses. They may explain what someone did, but that doesn't make them okay. You can't and won't be able to justify reactionary behavior, because as an adult you are responsible for your own behavior. No one makes you yell or slam a door. No one makes you ignore your partner. These are reactions to your emotions.

Assuming you agree with me that one of the big goals here is to have a healthy adult relationship with your partner, there is a certain belief you must adopt.

You cannot blame someone else for your behavior.

Of course, they can't blame you either. Getting blame out of your relationship is discussed in a later step because it does happen and it's a problem. Here I am simply saying that if you want a happy healthy secure relationship, you can't. You can't hit your partner over the head with a fish when you are upset and neither can partners blame the other for their own behavior.

You see, there is a point where they end and you begin. You are separate. You must hold on to yourself in the face of their reactions, otherwise you will do something to make it worse. This is called self-differentiation. Just because your partner may become reactionary doesn't mean you have to. Just because your partner is angry and raises their voice, doesn't mean it is okay

61

for you to call them an idiot. If you do, irrespective of what they might have done, you will have to own and repair your contribution. No one made you react, that's your stuff to work on.

Adults we respect and admire take ownership for their own behavior and don't blame it on anyone else. We try to teach our children that this is important too. When you express yourself through reactionary anger or withdrawal, you are not mindfully responding or managing yourself. Your child brain is taking over.

If you tend to express your emotions through reactive anger, you will most likely use criticism and contemptuous actions.

If you tend to shut down and withdraw, you will most likely use defensiveness and an "I am not going to deal with you" attitude. All of these wound your partner. They can't and won't be okay with these because of how these reactions impact them. Reactive behavior can and will eventually break your relationship.

Coping reactions in action

By now I hope you're seeing that one person's reactivity hurts the other person's feelings, which draws for a counter reaction. This becomes the negative cycle in your relationship. Let's run through an example of a cycle in slow motion so you can understand how this all weaves together. Then I'll show you how to quickly and easily make it short and clear. As we do this, keep in mind that:

When your attachment needs are not met,
your brain will activate emotions,
which then work to direct your behavior.

Let's say that being on time is really important to your part-ner. Let's also say you are running late to get ready to go some-where important to them. When they realize you are late, your partner will become internally agitated as they perceive a need of theirs not being met.

Since you are late and haven't acknowledged this, your part-ner's brain will conclude that they are not important to you. *Red alert!* It launches the emotional system to get them to act. They feel hurt.

Their hurt may consist of many pieces. Perhaps anger be-cause it feels unfair they managed their time to get ready and you didn't. They may feel powerless to get you to go faster. They might feel all alone in holding onto this important value, and alone in not feeling understood. They may feel scared that you will never meet their needs. With all these thoughts and feelings swirling inside like a cyclone in the tropics, chemicals are creat-ing an uncomfortable feeling inside their body. How well does their parent brain soothe or regulate their emotions?

If their parent brain can stay in charge and hold onto all the judgments and urges from the child brain, your partner might say, "Sweetie, I am a little frustrated that we're not running on time. Can I do anything to help you get ready faster?" This is a clear expression of their emotions and needs. It is a collaborative, non-blaming attempt to get you to be aware of their need and respond. The odds are far better of getting a helpful response when asking this way. Unfortunately in distressed relationships, emotions and needs sometimes don't come out in that helpful way, which is the reason for the distress. This is often because the child brain is running the show. So you get "What is the holdup here? Are you building the Great Wall of China on your face? Come on, we need to go."

That won't go very well at all. Nor does it work for your partner to ignore you the whole evening. Either way, their parent brain isn't strong enough or doesn't know how to step in and help the child brain cope, so those hurt feelings aren't managed well. Instead their hurt feelings probably come out in one of two ways: reactive anger or reactive withdrawal.

Now here is where things get worse. In response to your partner's attack, or withdrawal, what do you do? Do you meet fire with fire? "You're such a jerk! Quit yelling at me. I'll be ready whenever I feel like it!" Or do you shut down and ignore them for the next three hours? If so, your child brain is now running the show, too. It's a cycle you both contribute to.

So that's an example going in slow motion. Let's shorten it so you can work towards figuring out the cycle in your own relationship. This might be how you would talk to your partner about your frustration later on.

"When I see you are running late after we agreed on a time, I start to believe my need to be on time is unimportant to you; you don't care what is important to me. When I believe that, my feelings are hurt. What I do with that hurt is poke and jab at you. What I really need is for you to care more about what is important to me."

Here are more examples of negative cycles.

"When you get angry at me and yell, it is like a bomb going off. I immediately want to put my hands over my head and hide. I realize I have disappointed you again and just want to run away. When this happens I feel sad, alone, and scared. To cope with this, I move distant because I don't know what to do. What I really need from you is patience and understanding. I want you to see how hard I work, and if I am not doing it right, help me understand what you need, not just yell at me."

64

"When you come home from work and don't hug or talk to me, I start to believe that I am not important to you. Then I think that maybe you don't want to be with me and you don't love me. When this happens I feel sad and hurt. Instead of telling you this, I cope with that feeling by shutting down and avoiding you the rest of the evening. What I really need from you is to know you want to be with me and that you won't leave me."

"When I see you spending so much time working, I believe I am such a low priority; I feel hurt and abandoned. Instead of telling you this and asking for you to be with me, I cope with my hurt by criticizing how much time you spend working and demanding you work less. What I really need from you is to feel like I am more important."

The negative cycle in *your* relationship

Now that we have talked about needs, emotions, and reactions, we can finally put it all together. It is a negative cycle that invades *your* relationship. Here is a quick exercise to help you talk through and understand your own negative dance.

Below, put your relationship interactions into a cycle that you and your partner may be experiencing.

Fill in the following as though you were talking to your partner about your own experience:

When you _____ (what do you see or experience that hurts your feelings?), I start to believe that I am not _____ (which of the six attachment needs feels the most raw?).

Then I think thoughts such as _____ (list some of the thoughts you have and ones you think they have).

Then I feel _____ (mad, sad, scared, happy, what is the emotion you feel?).

Instead of telling you I am feeling _____ (the emotion), what I do to cope with that feeling is

_____ (what coping reaction do you commonly fall back on, or what do you do to self-soothe?).

What I really need from you is _____ (the more genuine need underneath all this).

Now go through this next paragraph and answer the way you believe your partner would if they were telling you about their experience. In other words, pretend to be them saying the following to you.

When you _____ (what do they see or experience that hurts their feelings?), I start to believe that I am not _____ (which of the six attachment needs do you think feels raw for them?).

I think thoughts such as _____ (list some of the thoughts you think they might have or they have said before).

Then I feel _____ (mad, sad, scared, happy, what emotion do you think they feel?).

Instead of telling you I am feeling _____ (the emotion), what I do to cope with that feeling is _____ (what coping reaction do they commonly fall back on, or what do you see them do to self-soothe? Hint: it is one that hurts your feelings).

What I think I really need from you is _____ (the more genuine need underneath all this).

If you are able to fill in these blanks for yourself and your partner, you are on your way to fixing your partner. Great job! Now it's time to start fixing things.

Time to break the negative cycle

The ten steps we are about to dig into will transform your relationship because they focus on two goals. First I we will cover the things to stop saying and doing that hurt. Then we will switch gears and put the focus on connection. In doing so we will work together on drawing your partner toward you for a closer and more secure relationship.

I realize that you may be doing this work alone. If this is the case, just follow the steps and you will be able to change your contribution to situations. This will change the experience your partner has with you and evoke a new response from them.

Remember humans are deeply motivated to get their needs met. When your partner needs you, they will be motivated to engage in a way that helps you continue to choose to be with them. This is my theory and one that has helped hundreds of couples in my practice. Now let's get from theory to practice, and start fixing your partner!

Chapter Takeaway:

When you express yours emotions through reactionary anger or by shutting down and withdrawing, you will get the opposite of what you really want.

Part 2
Stop the Insanity!

You've heard the saying, right? It is insanity to keep doing the same thing over and over, and expect a different result.

Maybe it will help if you raise your voice?

Chapter Six

Step 1
Build a Repair Kit

You can try and stuff all the hurts away into little
boxes and bury them somewhere deep inside you.
What happens, though, is at some point they begin to
leak out and poison your relationship.

"We fight, but nothing gets resolved." Sound familiar? In any relationship you are going to offend and be offended. Different values and competing needs will create fertile ground for misunderstandings to grow. It's going to happen. We just learned what happens when someone is offended, or hurt: they get emotional and sometimes reactive.

Ideally you would turn toward each other and receive soothing and comforting of your emotions. This is what repair brings and is a hallmark of a secure relationship. Without repair, without resolving issues, trust is difficult to nurture and connection is challenging to rebuild because the risk of being hurt again is too great.

Repair is critical to maintaining the trust and security of a relationship. Consider that if your partner doesn't understand

and own what they did to hurt your feelings, they might hurt you again. If they aren't sorry, they might hurt you again. If they don't commit to making a change and follow through with that change, you might get hurt again. When you are not able to rely on your partner to care about your feelings, to not hurt you, safety and trust are casualties. You are forced to build a wall to protect yourself. Repair must happen to keep you both connected and on the same page.

When hurts go unrepaired and get swept under the rug, partners lose some of the intimate connection that results from feeling emotionally safe. I see partners all the time who are struggling because their partner won't own their contribution and apologize. This is a huge problem, which is why I put it right up front in the *stop the insanity* part.

The truth is that it is hard to be vulnerable and intimate with someone who you believe might turn on you and hurt you. Without repair in a relationship, hurt feelings are not dissipated, so safety and trust are not regained. This will leave you disconnected and alone. Effective repair lays the groundwork for rebuilding trust and connection. The ability to repair hurts is a critical skill that couples must use continually.

Since the goal of the book is to fix your partner, let's be clear about the goal for this chapter on repair. I want to help you learn to approach your partner in a way that will evoke a helpful response in return.

This might mean you initiate repair and model what you want in the relationship. It might mean you express your need for them to better participate in repairing a hurt. Either way, you are going to be driving the bus through these ten steps, so buckle up.

Small, medium, and big hurts

Let's differentiate the types of hurts that can occur. Small hurts that happen between partners are like nicks and cuts to the relationship. Normally they cause very little emotional distress and are quickly repaired when acknowledged. If you are in the kitchen with your partner and they bump into you, the wound is pretty small. You probably just need a micro repair that looks like "Oops, I'm sorry." This is acknowledgment that you exist and you matter. If your partner asked you to iron their pants and you forgot, "Oh, I'm sorry I didn't get to them" will probably cover it along with some follow-through. *I'm sorry* needs to be part of your relationship along with *please* and *thank you* if you want to have a courteous and respectful one.

Small hurts are easy to roll through unless they are ignored. If there is no acknowledgment of the little offenses, they will accumulate and turn into medium hurts. You may have heard the term *death by a thousand paper cuts*? I think for relationships there is such a thing. Maybe you don't feel hurt each time your partner leaves their wet towel on the bed. Yet, if you ask them not to and they continue without ever offering an "I'm sorry," you will feel hurt.

Medium hurts usually result from the reactions that people have. These are things like name-calling, criticism, raised voices, sarcasm, and belittling. Moments that do not go well and escalate to this level of hurt require a little more effort to repair.

What if the hurt is not a scrape, but a knife in the back? Big hurts such as affairs, gambling away the retirement account, domestic violence—these are obvious betrayals of trust, ones that will require triage (prioritizing what to do in a crisis) and surgery. They necessitate a deep and sincere repair effort for the relationship to survive. Certainly these are crises and must be dealt with quickly and effectively. Big hurts like these require the full repair process. Partners must make changes in how they operate together in order to protect the relationship in the future.

Attachment injuries

Finally, there is a special kind of hurt that comes up in relationships. Attachment injuries often occur when you are feeling extremely vulnerable and reach for your partner. If they are not available and responsive, your brain registers this lack of response as dangerous to your survival in the moment.

Examples of this might be:

"When I went into the hospital for my surgery, you didn't visit because you were playing golf."

"When I was in the car accident, I called you and you didn't call me back."

"When my mother died and I was having a hard time, you just told me to get over it."

Notice the "I was alone and you were not here when I needed you" theme?

Many times someone experiencing this kind of hurt will conclude, *I cannot and will not ever risk reaching for them again.* This leads to you building a wall, strengthening that wall with resentment and maintaining a safe distance. Attachment injuries must be tended to with deep, sincere repair, continual reassurance, and follow-through of commitments to change. The good news is that no matter what size of hurt occurs, if you follow the repair model below, you have a great chance of getting through it and back to feeling good.

Who should go first?

The reality is that either one of you can go to the other and initiate repair at any time. The phone rings both ways, right? Moving towards your partner regardless of who feels more hurt or right is about prioritizing the relationship over either of you. Yes, I just suggested that the relationship is more important than either one of you. That may require sacrificing your ego if the relationship is suffering. With medium and bigger hurts, it makes sense for the person who feels more hurt to receive a bandage first. This is great when it works. However, since you're here to fix your partner, what if they are not very good at moving towards you to initiate repair?

My partner never apologizes

If you have a partner who doesn't usually (or ever) apologize, you will have to be the one to initiate repair first. Sorry, that's one of the "you have been elected, but didn't run for office" things. Of course, this may be something you want to see change in your relationship. If so, try modeling repair for a while. Then at some point in the near future, express the need you have for your partner to learn to initiate repair. When one partner has a lot of trouble owning their own behavior, it is typically related to their self-esteem. If deep down your partner fears they are not a good person, not lovable, or not competent, it is sometimes too painful for them to come to you and admit they made a mistake. Doing so would force them to touch and feel the sense of shame they already carry. Professional counseling might be helpful to enable your partner to move past this problem.

If you are the one who can't see any ownership to take in the situation, is it possible you at least feel badly that your partner feels hurt? If so then you could say, "I don't remember it that way, AND if that's how you saw it, I can see how that would hurt. I am so sorry for my part in this." The "and" is important because it acknowledges both sides without dismissing either. So even if you do not believe you really did or said what your partner believes that you did, you can still work on repair. Whatever you do, don't say, "I'm sorry you feel that way." That's just blaming them for their feelings and picking a fight.

If you can't do this, if you cannot find something to own or even feel badly when your partner is hurting, you might consider seeking a counselor. It might help you check out what's happening that you might not be seeing.

This could be especially helpful if you struggle with initiating repair. From what I have seen, when one partner believes the other will never own their behavior or apologize, distance and disconnection become a way to tolerate this unfairness. If you're willing to risk trying to initiate repair, that would be great. If not, a counselor may help you unpack your reasons and figure out how to work through this.

Avoid a "refight"

When they have an argument or experience a hurt, couples often try to work out the "facts" first. You might be interested to know that when we are in the midst of an argument and we're physiologically aroused into a fight-or-flight moment; your brain isn't good at keeping track of all the events. Nor are you able to be very empathetic because you're in survival mode. Couples who try to work out the "facts" often get stuck and start going back through past events trying to prove their points. That's a huge dead end.

If you can talk your way through the chain of events without the pokes and jabs at each other, it can work. However, if the conversation becomes about trying to get off the hook or shift responsibility, it will usually lead to defensiveness, dismissal, and denial. Now you're setting yourselves up for an escalation and a refight. To avoid this, always look for what you can own. Then, either one of you can move in with an "I'm sorry" at any time.

Acknowledging the other's hurt and offering a bandage soothes the escalating emotions and can keep you moving forward. It's sort of like helping make sure the other person doesn't drown while you're swimming back to shore after your boat sank. It's hard, but you have to look out for your partner.

Repair heals the relationship

Let's walk through the process of repair so you can see all the pieces, then we'll shorten it. When I gather myself up and move towards my wife (instead of staying in my man cave ignoring her) I to start the repair process. From this she will sense that she is important to me. Remember that being important is an attachment need, so by communicating this I help begin giving her relief from the emotional pain. I am communicating that I am looking out for her.

When I own what I did that hurt her, she will get a sense of being seen and understood. This looks like "I did yell at you when I was upset." When we fight, aren't we often trying to get the other person to see and own what they did that hurt us? When I own my contribution to her hurt, when I acknowledge what she is trying to get me to own, she won't have to keep fighting for me to understand her hurt.

Ideally when I own my part, I will include some empathy for

76

how this impacts her. This looks like "I know that hurts you." We will talk about empathy in detail; however, for now know that being empathetic helps you or your partner's brain shift out of a fight-or-flight zone. This happens because when you empathize with your partner, you are saying, *I see that you exist and see that your hurt is real for you.* When you or your partner can hear and feel this, a sense of acceptance and understanding exists, which are attachment needs. Meeting these needs soothes emotions.

A reasonable attempt to repair a medium or bigger hurt must include remorse. This looks like "I'm sorry." Simple, yet it is often missing. When you can express sincere remorse for your partner's hurt, you are being vulnerable with your partner. When you are genuine and vulnerable with your feelings instead of being reactive to them, your partner will often be drawn to protect you. They are compelled to step in and help you feel less crummy.

Next, I will need to make a promise to not hurt her in the future. This looks like "I promise not to yell at you, no matter how upset I get." How can you be close, vulnerable, and intimate with someone who you know is going to hurt you? You can't!

When you can offer a quality repair attempt that your partner soaks in and helps them feel better, they shift out of their fight-or-flight brain and back into where their thinking and reasoning brain is located.

Now they can see you are feeling bad, feel compassion, and ideally move in to offer some repair for their contribution. When that happens, you can both start feeling better and start healing as a couple. When you do start feeling better, more aligned and connected again, it is not uncommon for couples to have "makeup sex" at that point. Sex, for many people, particularly men, communicates acceptance. If a hurt partner will have sex with the one who has hurt them, it feels as though at a deep level *I am still accepted, we are still okay, we are going to make it.* Phew! Now doesn't that feel better?

Four steps to proper repair

In my work with couples who are dealing with lots of hurts, I have seen plenty of attempts at repair. Some are good, but many fall flat because the person attempting repair skips steps or even hijacks the repair by talking about them self. There are four specific components of repair that must happen for it to be effective. Micro repairs or the small hurts that just need an "Oops, sorry, sweetie" don't always need the full meal deal here. Everything else, though, needs a proper repair experience, or it will keep coming up like sardines for lunch.

Let's build your first aid kit with the critical parts of repair. This chapter is a bit longer than the others because repair has four steps to get through. Once you see the pattern, you'll realize these make sense and are easy to remember.

1. Take ownership for the part that caused a hurt

There is something relieving about hearing another person who has caused hurt acknowledge that hurt. We all need validation. It's really quite simple. When you acknowledge a hurt you caused, your partner will get a sense of being understood, which is an attachment need. Instinctively their brain recognizes that if you know what you did, there is a good chance you may not do it to them again.

Ownership is not about accepting blame for everything, nor is it about owning something you didn't do. Often what you will

78

need to own is your reactive behavior. Being upset is okay, but tossing the remote control at the TV is not okay. If you did, you'll have to own that. When you own your part, the path will be clear for your partner to own their side of the hurt. Of course, you want to create a relationship where they own their stuff, too. For now you're modeling this.

Since communication is everything, the words you choose matter. As such, there is one important note I want to make about taking ownership: there are no *buts*. "I'm sorry, *but* . . ." is not ownership; it is defensiveness and shifting blame. Just don't speak it, or you will completely sabotage your efforts.

Here is what taking ownership looks like:

> "Yes, I did _____."
> "I did stay out past the agreed time."
> "I did not check in with you."
> "I did walk away when you were still talking to me."
> "I did miss that you were tearful and needed my support."

Many people try to make it conditional or include blame.

"I'm sorry you didn't like it when I _____." This is not taking ownership; it is blaming the other person for what they feel.

"I'm sorry you feel that way." This is a classic reply that is neither taking ownership nor an apology. Again, *it is blaming*.

"I'm sorry, but I was just trying to _____." Yikes, there is that "B" word. Can you feel how it is dismissive? When you use the word "but," you are saying, *forget everything I just said, here is what I really think.* The best advice here is not to stick your "but" into an apology.

Remember that you do not have to apologize for the *feelings*

79

you have. It's what you *do with* your feelings, how you express those emotions, that is usually the source of the hurt.

"When we were fighting, I did slam the door and call you names." That's ownership. That is stepping up to acknowledge what your partner might have found hard or hurtful.

"I did take the money from savings without talking to you first." "I did get a little flirtatious with that waitress." "I did forget to call you after I left work." "I did tell you I would take you to dinner instead of going to the game." These are all clear acknowledgments of the cause of someone's hurt. Look for that kernel of truth in what you might have done that your partner is having a problem with, and highlight that piece by taking ownership.

You might be wondering how you can take ownership for something you don't agree is wrong. Sometimes you might believe you acted justly or made the right decision, particularly if you had a good intention. Yet, your partner is still saying they are hurt. If you find yourself in this spot, remember this saying:

Being right has no place in a close relationship.

You can be "right" all day long and quickly find yourself alone. Winning an argument or being right is just about getting yourself off the hook. You can sometimes do that, but I think it's a zero-sum game. If you are right, your partner has to be wrong, and I promise that won't help them move toward you to meet your needs. Instead look for that kernel of truth in what they say has hurt them; look for the contribution you had, no matter how small. In this first step I'm not suggesting you are agreeing to

80

change anything. You're simply saying, "I see that what I did has hurt you."

Taking ownership of your part, even any part, of the hurt will give your partner the validation they want and need. If they've been fighting to get you to see their side, this communicates, "Yes, I now see that I did contribute to your hurt feelings." This is a big part of what your partner needs to get some relief and feel calm again.

2. Express remorse

After taking ownership, it is time to express remorse. This is a necessary piece because if your partner doesn't express remorse, they might offend again. In that case, how can you trust again? Expressing remorse actually means saying the words "I am sorry." Ideally it will include a little validation for the hurt it caused: "I know that hurts you."

The bigger the hurt, the more an expression of remorse is required. As I said, the small boo-boos often just need a little acknowledgment of remorse, a little micro repair like "Oh, I am so sorry I didn't call you back after my meeting." You may not actually feel a lot of remorse here; the offense was small, so the emotions are small. It's mostly about acknowledging the other's feelings. This is often all the small hurts need to be fixed.

A medium hurt, big hurt, or attachment injury needs more attention. Maybe think of it as the amount of time and energy you want to spend on a repair being in direct proportion to the offense. If you gamble away all the grocery money for the month, "Oops, I'm sorry" probably won't cut the mustard. You will want to spend more time and energy communicating that you actually feel a sense of remorse.

The expression of remorse doesn't have to come with tears; however, tears are often a sign of vulnerability. It is that vulnerability that the repair needs to work. This is why when one partner will never apologize for their behavior, there will be a lot of hurts swept under the rug. Where you find those, you will often find resentment, low trust, and disconnected partners.

What if you don't feel remorseful?

What if you really believe that you are right? What if you don't believe your partner *should* have hurt feelings? Repair isn't about pointing fingers; it is not about taking all the blame. Repair is about "I see that you are hurt, and I want to help us both feel better."

A way to say that is, "Wow, if you heard me say that, I don't blame you for being upset. I am so sorry." Or, "I don't remember doing that, but if you believe I did then I can understand how upset you would be. I am so sorry this happened." Can you see here how you can still offer repair even if you do not believe you did anything wrong?

I understand that there are many variables that can go into a situation. Much of the discussion prior to the repair attempt is about trying to understand what each of you experienced and are thinking and feeling as a result. Repair happens for real once you can identify your ownership or contribution to the hurt.

When you can find something to own, when you can look at your partner and say "I'm sorry" and genuinely mean it. This helps you are communicate, *You are important to me, and I see I have disappointed you. I do not want to let you down because you matter to me.*

These are the underlying messages that get conveyed in a

quality repair effort. These help heal the attachment bond that has been injured. Expressing a sense of remorse is part of that healing.

3. Make a new commitment

If you have gotten here by going through the first two steps, I would say the hardest part is over. I see partners go here right away, skipping the ownership and remorse part. That will completely dismiss your partner's emotions, which will torpedo the repair effort.

Earlier I said that when you take ownership, you are not yet agreeing to change anything. Now is the moment where you commit to some change that will protect you, your partner, and your relationship from re-experiencing the hurt again. What will be different as a result of suffering this hurt? This is where you forge the new agreement and start feeling like you're back on the rails.

Keep in mind there are probably two tracks to cover here. First, if you are repairing a hurt caused because you were reactive during a disagreement or misunderstanding (slamming the door, calling them names, refusing to talk about something), your new commitment will be specifically around that behavior.

Second, there is still the other conversation to have about the problem itself. The initial repair around reactivity is an attempt to put the rules of safe engagement back in place that allow couples to talk about the issue that caused it in the first place. Now you have to deal with the original hurt.

Let's say that you come home after work only to find your partner is gone without a note. Three hours later when the clock hits midnight, you are worried and angry; you are feeling unimportant and unappreciated. You head off to bed, but not before shutting the power off to the garage door so they can't get in the house.

When you eventually work on repairing all this, at some point it will be your turn to repair your part. Usually you first have to get through the reactionary stuff that made it worse. In this case it looks like "I did shut off the power in the garage, and I am sorry I did that to you. If I get upset again, I will not lock you out."

Note that all three steps were included: ownership, an expression of remorse, and a new commitment. Now you have to talk about the problem; going out without letting the other person know where and when you'll be home.

Warning: this is often a place where fights erupt again. This happens not necessarily because two people cannot agree, but because the negative cycle of emotions and reactions starts up around that topic or issue. Someone says something critical or gets defensive, the magical spell of repair and connection is broken, and both partners pick up their boxing gloves again.

If you are working on modeling repair and don't yet have your partner on board, first initiate repair by owning your part. It is imperative that you stay calm and collaborative. If things escalate, either of you might need a break of thirty minutes or more to calm down and think about how you feel and what you need.

This third step in the repair process must address what you are going to do differently. "Next time I will _____." What will you do to address the hurt so that it doesn't keep happening? Talk about it, negotiate, double-check that your partner believes it will work for them. The new commitment has to be doable for both of you. That brings us to the final step.

4. Make amends—take action & follow through

Trust is a common casualty of the hurts that befall relationships. As you might imagine, it is a very common conversation in couples counseling. How do you get trust back? Let me give you a very simple and clear definition of trust.

Trust is promises made, promises kept consistently over time.

When you make a new commitment that your partner accepts as part of the repair process, they are basically agreeing that "Yes, if you do what you have now committed to, I can move forward in the relationship."

You won't be able to do this with only words in the moment. Step three sets the intention; step four is where the rubber hits the road and you prove that your words and emotions were sincere.

Making amends can also mean taking action to show you are truly sorry. If I promise my wife I won't be late to pick her up from work again and then leave her sitting on the curb waiting for thirty minutes, she will be hurt and upset and lose some trust in me. I have to follow through with the commitment I made to gain her trust back.

To "put back in" or make amends, I might also want to take her to dinner, buy her flowers, or make some other gesture to demonstrate that I feel bad and want her to feel better and trust me.

That is part of the dance couples do to continue communicating, "You are important to me, I understand I hurt you, I appreciate you accepting me again, I want to feel close to you, and I want you to think I'm a good person." A simple gesture of amends can mean a lot. Reoffending can take it all away and dig a deeper hole.

What if they don't follow through?

When someone says they are sorry and promises to be different but then doesn't follow through, trust is broken, sometimes into even more pieces. This is the dangerous part because if there is no follow-through, future efforts to repair will fail. Underneath all this, if the injuring partner does not follow through, they will be communicating, *I didn't really mean what I said. Your hurt is not so important to me that I will change. You are not important to me.*

If someone doesn't follow through and trust is broken yet again, all four repair steps must still happen. This has to be managed like any other hurt. This means initiating a conversation and a repair attempt that follows these steps.

Keep this model of repair handy. Being in relationships, and being around other humans, you are bound to experience hurt feelings. The ability to repair and heal is critical in any relationship. To do this, remember the four steps.

Repair is:
1. Taking ownership
2. Expressing remorse
3. Making a new commitment
4. Making amends / following through

Step 1

Experiment for This Step

Model the changes you want in the relationship by being the first one to pull out the repair kit. When your partner seems to be upset, frustrated, or hurt, it is your moment to be there for them.

Since you are their partner, by being in the relationship you have already agreed to this. Move in as soon as possible with a repair effort that follows the first three repair steps and then follow through to build trust. If it fails, wait for a bit and try again with, "I don't want to fight with you. Can we talk?"

How to initiate repair with your partner

First, focus on repairing the micro hurts. If you are interacting with your partner and bump into them, make sure you say, "Oops, sorry, sweetie. I didn't mean to bump you." If you notice they are a little hurt, frustrated, irritated, or annoyed, or seem defensive, jump in with a quick "Whoops, I'm sorry, I didn't mean to upset you." Know it is usually okay to be curious too. "Hey, did I do something to upset you?" These little moments of soothing are cues that say, *I notice you and care that you might be hurting.*

Next, when there is a bigger hurt between you that needs repair, *even if you didn't cause that hurt,* you can still move toward your partner to help by initiating repair. "I don't like fighting with you. Do you want to talk?" Or, "Can we try and repair things?"

Make sure your partner is willing to hear you by inviting them into the conversation. "I would really like to repair this. Can we talk?" If accepted, go sit somewhere without distractions, try to understand their side of things *by listening* about where they feel hurt, and then follow the four steps.

In a healthy adult relationship, partners are working to care for, not hurt, each other. You initiating repair first may seem like you're falling on the sword, but in doing so you are prioritizing the relationship above your own needs and modeling what you want your partner to be willing to do also.

If you cannot see your part of the hurt, remember that everything is cause and effect. Back up in the chain of events leading up to the hurt. Often, someone is upset from an earlier hurt, and it infects the current moment. Go back to an earlier point of the day and then move forward step by step, considering how your actions may have impacted your partner. If you just can't see it, ask your partner. "I want to take responsibility for what I did that was hard for you. Help me understand where your feelings were hurt." Most likely you'll find something you did, and can use that in your repair effort.

Help your partner repair with you

It would be easy to just sit back and let your partner move toward you to repair all the hurts. Since you are here reading my book, I'm going to run with the belief that your partner doesn't do that. Waiting for your partner to move toward you puts you in a powerless position and sets you up for disappointment, but what can you do?

If you need an "I'm sorry" from them, you are going to have to ask for it. This might feel unfair, and yet I wager that you will feel better than if you wait around feeling disappointed and unimportant. The catch is that if you are going to ask for what you need (something I encourage); you are responsible for how you approach them. If they feel blamed, shamed, criticized, or attacked, they will just get defensive and you won't get what you need. Here are some examples of how to initiate asking for them to repair something.

"I really need to talk about what happened yesterday. Can you do that now or when would you be willing?"

"I am still upset about this morning, and I don't want to be. I need to talk about things. When can we do that?"

Once you are to the point when you've both talked about what happened and you are ready for them to repair, ask for it. "For me to feel better, I need to hear that you understand me and that you are sorry."

I completely get that asking for this won't feel as good as if they offer it on their own. We're working on changing things; for now that means taking the first step to model the way you want the relationship to be.

Having a good repair kit is the first step. Now let's work on reducing the need to use it. Step two is about stopping the misunderstandings.

Chapter Seven

Step 2
Stop the Misunderstandings

No one has a crystal ball. Help your partner to better understand what you want and why, and you will dramatically improve your chances of getting it.

This may or may not surprise you, but a great many couples that come into my office looking for help with an argument find that the root problem was caused by a misunderstanding. How many times did you have a fight, only later to figure out it all stemmed from a simple, avoidable misunderstanding? Misunderstandings often happen because we misinterpret our partner's intentions. If only they would make their intentions more clear. This is the goal for step two.

Understanding the communication gap

A man named Bob Wallen created a fantastic communication model for understanding the idea that intentions do not always match up with the impact on others. He calls this problem the Interpersonal Gap ("INTERPERSONAL GAP"; Robert Wallen). This gap can be summarized by saying,

We know ourselves by our intentions, and we know others by their actions and words.

To know others, you have to use a filter to make an interpretation, an assumption, about their intention. You know the joke about how assumptions "make an ass out of u and me," right? The difference between what your intentions are and what your partner assumes your intentions to be becomes the communication gap between you.

Let's say that on Saturday morning I wake up and start working on the household finances. This means I have to categorize expenses for the week. If I go to my wife with one of the receipts from her weekly shopping and ask her the question "Why did you spend eighty-five dollars at the department store? What was this for?" I am potentially picking a fight. She will probably assume I am about to sit in judgment of her purchase.

In asking that question, I haven't really expressed what my intentions are. I haven't let her know my motivation for asking about the receipt. Yet, in order for her to respond, she will first need to decode my question and determine what information I am actually looking to acquire.

All of us have a filter composed of all our life experiences, especially with the person we are interacting with in the moment. Our brain will also include our innate needs in that moment along with the potential interpersonal consequences of both the other's question and our potential responses. This may seem complicated, but don't worry, there is an easy way out.

Leading with your intention

Thankfully there is a ridiculously easy way to manage this problem and avoid many of the misunderstandings that can and do occur. The solution here is to *lead with your intention*. Explain up front the why behind your statement or question. Communicating with your partner means that as you speak, you are mindful of how what you are saying or asking will impact them. Do this always and I sincerely mean always. Leading with your intention will show that you are considerate of your partner and that you are not expecting them to read your mind. Asking questions that pull for information without a clear intent will feel manipulative and tick your partner off.

Not: "Why are you wearing that shirt?" Instead, "I was looking forward to dressing up together. Would you be okay wearing a nicer shirt?"

Not: "I am hungry." How about "I am hungry and wondered if you would make me a sandwich?"

Not: "What time are you leaving?" Try "I wasn't sure if I had time to run to the store before you go. What time are you leaving?"

In expressing your main goal, reason, motivation, or need underneath your statement or question, you bring more clarity to the moment; you make more sense. However, this means you have to actually be aware of what you want or need. Identifying your need and expressing it clearly helps you maintain your personal power. When you lead with your intention, you are working to help the other person better understand what you are saying or asking of them. This enables your partner to engage and respond to you more effectively. Yes, I am suggesting it is mostly your responsibility as the speaker, in any moment, to say what you need in a way the other person can understand. If you want to evoke a better response from your partner, limit their need to run your words and intentions through their filters. Limit their need to make assumptions by helping them understand what it is you actually want from them.

To close that gap of understanding with my wife in regards to the receipt, I would do better to ask my question by leading with my intention. "I am working to categorize our expenses from the week. I'm not sure where this goes. What was the eighty-five dollars for at the department store?"

Feels better, doesn't it? Now my wife knows what my needs are and what information I am actually looking to receive from her. She knows how to meet my needs and answers the question in a way that moves us forward. Even more important, I have taken a moment to consider how my words might impact her, and by being clear, I have protected her from being hurt by my words.

Shooting questions at her without explaining my intention will just feel like an interrogation. If I am unhappy about her spending money, then I need to say so. I could invite her into a conversation to create a new understanding and agreement. That would look like "I don't know what this is for and worry that you're spending money we haven't agreed upon. Can you share with me what this was for so I can understand?" That might launch a difficult conversation, but at least you are clear with your feelings and intention and avoid going on the attack.

I once had a couple in my office. The wife talked about her interest in signing up for a one-hundred-mile bicycle ride. Her husband commented, "If you did that, I would be proud of you." A seemingly nice reply, yet she admitted to being offended and launched a few defensive comments in return.

As we dissected what had just happened, she opened up about having a lack of confidence in herself. She carried the deep belief that she had not accomplished much in life and feared her partner felt the same about her. With all this going on, the comment "If you did that, I would be proud of you" was decoded as sarcastic and was taken by her to mean something closer to "If you did that, I would finally have a reason to be proud of you, because up until now you have been a loser." Yikes, if that's what she thought she heard, no wonder she became defensive!

After we talked about her beliefs and emotions that came from her not feeling good about herself, I suggested she ask what her partner's intention was in making the comment. Seeking clarity of intention is always useful. Her husband said he was surprised that his intention to be supportive was taken as a put-down. He stepped up to repair this by reassuring her that his intentions were coming from a place of pride he already had for her, not criticism. She then stepped in to acknowledge that she made assumptions based on how she felt about herself.

The end result was that both of them felt better. We then talked about how easily even a well-intended comment can turn into hurt feelings and a fight. Only through more clear intention and inquiry can you protect yourself and the relationship from a poor outcome. We are all busy decoding what we see and hear, but not always being clear about or clarifying the intention behind our own words and actions.

Over Communicate

Using more words to be clear about your intention may seem like over communicating (is that possible?), and may feel mechanical at first, yet leading with your intention can magically grease the communication channel. Remember, you are here reading this book because you are struggling to communicate. If you want to improve your communication, I suggest you need to do something different.

We often work harder to make our intention clear when we know the other person may not understand what we want to say

or ask. However, in our relationship with our partner, we sometimes assume they have a crystal ball and just know what we're
thinking. When they don't, we get frustrated. This is why leading
with your intention is so important. Here are a few more examples:

Don't ask, "What time are you coming home?" This might be
taken as judgmental or controlling and put your partner on edge.
Instead say, "I'm going to be cooking dinner tonight. Can you let
me know what time you are planning to be home?"

Not: "Why are you doing it that way?" *Why* is a critical and
judgmental word. When you ask "why," your partner may inter-
pret this as you saying, "You are an idiot for making the decision
to do it that way." *Why* is one word couples need to eliminate
from their vocabularies. It really says, "What is wrong with you
that you did it that way?" Instead, how about "When you do it
that way, I'm worried about _____." This more clearly expresses the impact on you in a way they can respond to.

Step 2

Experiment for This Step

One of the reasons couples struggle is that each partner starts falling into a rigid and predictable pattern of responses. Have you ever found yourself saying, *I don't bother talking to my partner because I know exactly how it will go*? Assuming that a certain outcome will always occur means you are curbing your own behavior. You are basing your actions on assumptions and not giving your relationship a chance to grow.

While working through all these steps and experiments, try this: Deliberately avoid anticipating the outcome. Decide not to let past experiences poison your efforts. With each experiment, be curious, reflect how it goes, and tweak it for next time. Change won't be instant, yet even small changes can help things feel better fast. Let's try making sure your intentions are more clear and see what happens.

Lead with your intention

Lead with your intention when you make statements or ask questions. Use the words "My intention is _____" to help you get in the habit of thinking this way. "My intention here is to try and be helpful so you get done faster and we can go eat sooner. Would you like some help with this?" "My intention is to repair this hurt because you are important to me." "My intention is to plan out our day because I want to be sure we can spend time together." These extra words help your partner avoid having to fill in the gaps with negative stories about your intention.

If you are asking a question, convey what information you are trying to piece together. State up front why a question you are asking is important to you. Be clear about what will you do with the information they give you.

Not: "What is your schedule this weekend?" Instead try "I have a question. My intention is to try to figure out if we have time to go to my mom's on Saturday. What are your plans for this weekend?"

I know it takes extra words to keep your partner up to speed with the context of your statement and questions. They won't be consulting a psychic to analyze all your thoughts and meanings so you might as well share them up front. If you are conversing and you notice your partner looks confused (good job for noticing), ask them. "I notice you are looking confused. My intention here is to get on the same page. Do you need me to clarify something?" This will initially seem as though you are over communicating, yet if you are struggling to communicate, this little tool might be exactly what you need to create a better way of being together. What feels like over communicating might actually be the right amount. You're just not used to it.

I am willing to bet leading with your intention will quickly help reduce the number of misunderstandings and friction points you have and help your relationship start feeling better quickly.

This is exactly why I put this step near the top of the list. I think you are going to find this a great way to start fixing your partner.

Help your partner clarify their intention

If your partner makes a statement or asks a question, notice if their intention is clear or not and how you feel if you don't understand it. If that happens, know it is okay to ask them to clarify. However, in asking them for clarity, be sure and clarify your intention for asking first.

Let's say they ask you, "What are your plans?" If you answer with "Why are you asking?" it won't go over well. You've just asked the "why" question as well as answered their question with a question, which usually irks people because it feels like deflection. Instead say, "I'm not sure what you need here. Do you want my schedule for the whole day or just the morning's schedule?" Work to help them be more clear, but first state your intention to help. "I want to help you, I'm just confused. Are you talking about this weekend or next?" It's okay to ask them, nicely of course, what they need in that moment.

Missing intentions aren't the only things that cause fights. Deep in every human psyche is the desire to be free. When you take away your partner's freedom expect them to be defiant. In step three, we'll take a look to see if that's happening in your relationship, and if so, fix it.

Chapter Eight

Step 3
Stop Being a Dictator

When I hear you tell me to do this or don't,
I feel an "F you" coming on.

How do you react when someone tells you what to do or what not to do?

"Go get me a glass of water."

"Don't touch that."

"Take the garbage out."

"You need to stop spending so much time watching TV." Do you feel compelled to comply or resist?

Me, I get a little charge in my body when I hear this. My thoughts go something like: "Stop telling me what to do. I will do what I want, when I want. Wait until you see me NOT do what you want. That'll teach you!" Admittedly there might be a few flavorful adjectives in there as well. This happens because:

No one likes to be told what to do.

The fight for freedom

We all have an innate desire to be free deep in our human DNA. Freedom is a much-cherished concept, the fight for which has been woven into human history since day one for a reason. Human beings crave freedom from others and control of their own lives. When our freedom feels challenged, we resist with everything we've got. No wonder much of the conflict inherent in relationships revolves around the fight for connection and the fight for independence. We exist in the tension between our individuality and the partnership.

I'm sure you have experienced this. When your partner communicates their needs to you in a way that feels like a command or demand, don't you feel the deep, primal urge to resist or protest? "Pick up your coat." "You need to take the dog for a walk." Even if you choose to meet the demand made, often it will be out of resentment or guilt. When those feelings pressurize like lava in a volcano, eventually an eruption will follow.

How we treat each other matters.

Our goal here is to approach our partner in a way that evokes a response in return that feels good. If we use words designed to pick fights, whose fault is it? If you are commanding and demanding of your partner, you are picking a fight and that's yours to own.

"You need to empty the dishwasher." "Here, take this." "Hand me that." All without a *please* or *thank you*. If you hear your partner express their wants and needs in this way, are you motivated to comply with joy in your heart? I doubt it.

I sometimes ask couples to ponder the question "How do you treat the person you love the most in the world?" My answer is, gently, with kindness and consideration. My wife has a great image for this. She suggests that for me to approach her to get my needs met, I approach her like a feather, not a hammer. That's a work in progress for me because habits are hard to break, but you know what? The feather works better!

Ironically, when we are out in public, with friends, or at work, we are all magically more polite. At a dinner party we might say, "Would you please pass me the salt?" then follow up with "Thank you." At the grocery store if someone stopped to help us pick up an item we dropped, we would say, "Thank you so much. I appreciate your help." We express kindness, consideration, and appreciation for strangers.

You are here reading this book because you want your relationship to feel better. You want to be happier and have a kinder and more loving partner. You want to fix your partner, which in this chapter means you will stop telling them what to do, and handle it differently when they tell you what to do. This means: be the change you want. Model the changes and way of being that you want your partner to follow in the relationship.

There are no demands or commands
in relationships, only requests and favors.

Communicating with your partner, or anyone, is usually about trying to get them to meet a need or want you have. Because what you say and how you say it matters, it is important to be mindful of your approach. If you phrase everything you ask for as a favor, you are giving your partner the power and freedom to comply. A command or demand takes their desire away.

When someone we care about asks for a favor, don't we usually feel a desire to be helpful? When someone who means a lot to us asks for help, we usually want to respond from a place of love and joy. We want to nurture the relationship, and give so as to maintain and strengthen the trust and connection.

The next time you need to ask your partner for something, be mindful of how you ask. Increase the odds that they will comply by considering the words you use and how you use them. Use a softer voice, lead with your intention, and ask for a favor. "I am hungry and only have twenty minutes to get ready for work. Would you do me a favor and make me a sandwich?"

Send cues of love with your request

When you want or need something, it helps to express it in a way that draws out a positive response. I encourage couples to use terms of endearment. When your partner hears "honey," "sweetie," "babe," or whatever softer terms have become part of your relationship, your partner may feel softer too. It is hard to attack someone who is being kind and gentle. This isn't about acting like a lost puppy and tugging at their heartstrings. That would be guilt and manipulation, which is not what I am advocating. By using a term of endearment and asking as a favor, not commanding, I suggest you are offering more love and respect. If you do not have pet names or terms of endearment, I suggest adding them to your repertoire. If you don't like them, learn to speak their first name in a way that creates a sense of love and closeness. This becomes a verbal cue to their brain that care is being expressed. It prepares our brain to receive something loving. Just don't use it ONLY when you want a favor, or they'll see it as manipulation and get upset. Use it to express your love too to help create the association with affection and softness.

What if you are upset or angry?

If you find yourself upset with your partner and needing to ask for something, it is still up to you to manage your emotions. Just because you are upset doesn't mean it is okay to become a drill sergeant or be mean. If you did, that would be you reacting versus managing yourself and your emotions

"Take out the trash" can still be "Honey, could you do me a favor and take out the garbage?" "Get your wet towel off the bed" would still be "Sweetie; I really don't like it when you leave your wet towel on the bed. Can you please put it into the laundry basket?" Using a term of endearment, or at least asking for a favor, will communicate to them that you are managing your emotions. You are keeping the emotional safety in the relationship by saying, *Even though I am upset, I still love and respect you.*

I know, I know. You're feeling all soft and wimpy by using all these fluffy words, yet be honest. Can you feel the difference? If those softer words were coming your way, would you feel a greater desire to comply? We are trying to help you get your partner to respond more appropriately and effectively. We want them to hear your words and respond not just feel defensive and blame you for being angry or critical. What you say and how you say it matters.

Step 3

Experiment for This Step

Make requests. Ask for favors. Add a term of endearment to those requests. Don't forget to lead with your intention.

To get your partner to respond more often with less resistance to your expressed needs, you have to help them feel good about helping.

Make a request that works

Start with a term of endearment (pet name) or use their name warmly, be clear with your intention, and make your request.

"Hey, honey, I'm trying to get the cupboard organized. Can you do me a quick favor?" Be aware of your tone of voice, body language, and facial expressions. Yes, I know it is hard. If you flub it up and they grow a grumpy look on their face, or even snap back, you'll have to own your contribution.

"I'm sorry, I got a little frustrated and took it out on you." That would be a way for you to care for your partner while still acknowledging and managing your emotions.

"David, I am worried about getting done in time. It would be great if you could help me for a minute."

"Sweetheart, I wanted to get dinner started. Do you have any idea what time you'll be able to come home to eat?"

Help your partner make requests

If your partner tends to be demanding and commanding, and you want to change this in your relationship, your first step is to model what you want. Don't be guilty of being demanding to them.

The next step is to be aware of your own fight-or-flight response. It is common for many of us to feel as though Mom or Dad is ordering us around again. If this happens to you, remember this:

You don't have to accept every invitation to fight. Learn how to decline with grace.

The next time they foist their demands upon you, first take a breath to let the urge to fight flow through you. Then open with whatever sincere term of endearment you might use, without being sarcastic. Finally, be clear with your intention and try giving them a little gentle feedback. It takes longer to explain than say it! Here is what it looks like:

"Sweetie, I would love to do that for you, and I will. Can you just please ask me instead of ordering me?" Then walk away and do it. Remember, you have to be sure you are working to make requests and not demands of them first. Don't let yourself fall into being hypocritical. Now let's get to one of the most common problems in relationships and make sure you're not *shoulding* on your partner.

Chapter Nine

Step 4
Stop *Shoulding* on Your Partner

"Should" is a violent word. It takes away the other
person's autonomy and independence.

When trying to express their need or perhaps a frustration about something you did or didn't do, does your partner *should* on you? "You *should* get to the gym more." "You *shouldn't* drink so much." "You *should* call me when you are going to be home late." Does it feel like you just don't measure up or do it *right* in their eyes?

When you share something from your day, does your partner try to fix you? "You *should* tell your boss you aren't going to do that." "You know what you *should* do, just tell them you are taking the day off." Do you feel belittled or thought of as being incapable? The word *should* is part of that "demanding and commanding" repertoire that people use to express their thoughts, feelings, and needs.

The impact, however, is more like unwanted advice. It leaves you feeling less than, or incapable. Worse, without empathy you'll get that sense of not being understood and certainly not feel close. *Shoulding* is basically judgment and criticism, and these are big problems in relationships.

Sometimes *should* is used as a defense to avoid owning one's behavior. For example, if your partner brings up a problem and then you say, "You *should* have checked first, and then we wouldn't be in this mess." This is criticism with blame. "If you loved me, you wouldn't do that." This is manipulative via an unstated *you shouldn't do that* statement. Neither is helpful.

If your partner is *shoulding* you, the issue here is twofold. First, if they think you *should* and you didn't, or if they think you *shouldn't* and you did, it means they will be disappointed and upset. In reality this is caused by their own expectations of you.

Secondly, *should* is by its very nature judgmental and critical. *Should* points out your shortcomings and failures—in their mind. It does not help you to feel connected or motivated to be responsive. Instead you'll just feel put down and *not good enough*. The *shoulds* comes from one's judgment and are communicated through criticism, which no one likes to receive.

No one likes to be judged

To our brain, *judging* is part of the necessary processing we do to form an opinion about an issue. Judgment can be good, like when we judge someone as doing a great job. This is called a compliment and is usually welcome.

When we *judge* someone, it is because we see them as falling short in our eyes. When we believe someone else is judging us, it taps into the part of us that fears, "I am not good enough."

Whatever you think in your mind is yours to think; however,

if you outwardly communicate to your partner, *I judge you as a failure*, don't be shocked when they become defensive and upset. It simply hurts to be criticized, so don't!

Criticism

Shoulds, or judgment, are often communicated through criticism. It is imperative that you get criticism out of your relationship. Criticizing your partner takes the attention off the issue or problem behavior and turns that focus onto their personality or character.

When we are criticized or belittled, we feel put down and blamed. Criticism communicates that there is but one right way to do things. *You are a disappointment; you did it wrong, so therefore you are worthless. You are not good enough.* Those are painful messages that bore down into your partner's self-esteem and self-confidence. Not helpful stuff if you were hoping to snuggle on the couch later.

Criticism is a tool used to get another person to comply. That's why a *should* feels critical. Think of critical comments as verbal cattle prods. If your partner steps out of line or breaks the rules and you give them a zap with a critical comment, don't be surprised if they attack back. When you or your partner relies on criticism as an attack or defensive response, it will infect your cycle of communication and poison your connection.

Ironically the desire to be connected is what gives criticism the power to work. We typically don't want to disappoint our partner, so we eventually work harder to avoid the upset that seems to surround their critical *you should*. However, when a criticized partner starts to feel hopeless about pleasing the other, they lose that desire to connect at all.

Individuals can go into a relationship with good self-esteem and come out a wreck because of continual criticism, which is constant rejection of them as a person by someone they allowed themselves to become vulnerable to. Obviously not a recipe for love and intimacy.

Criticism destroys self-esteem

Criticism rarely leads to effective change because giving in to criticism means submitting to the will of the other while being devalued. No one likes to feel devalued and forced to submit to another. Criticism is a put-down and leads to feeling blamed. This evokes defensiveness, feelings of unworthiness, which fuels resentment, and disconnection, which can lead to the end of a relationship. Yes, criticism is powerful enough, over time, to bring on that result. Being criticized all the time will either feed into or even create low self-esteem. Having a low self-esteem is like not having any skin—everything hurts. Humans can only take so much hurt and pain until leaving the relationship is a better option, *no matter what the cost.*

Constructive criticism is just feedback, right?

No it is not. My wife is a parent coach and child therapist working to help children and families get along better. She often says that "criticism has no place in families or relationships." You may wonder, then, how can you give feedback in your relationship? The truth is that sometimes you do need to explain to your partner that they are not meeting your needs in some way. However, you have a responsibility to express yourself in a way that they can hear. You have to be soft, or they will only see your anger and feel their pain. Remember: there are no demands, only requests, in relationships.

"You always leave the cereal on the counter" is not feedback, it is criticism. It really says, "You are such a lazy bum, you left the cereal on the counter again."

An expression of need that feels much better would be "Hey, I noticed the cereal was out on the counter. Can you do me a favor and work on putting it back?" Or if you are dealing with a child or teen, get up and hand them the cereal so that it is a reminder for them to follow through. *You are trying to train not shame them.* "Hey, would you mind getting the dishes into the dishwasher? Thanks." That's better then, "How many times do I have to ask you to put the dishes in the dishwasher?" Feel the shame being delivered?

Stop *shoulding* by eliminating toxic words

To stop *shoulding*, to reduce the judgment, to quit criticizing, to improve your chance at better communication, removing a few key words from your vocabulary will do wonders. Remember, you are trying to "fix" your partner by changing how you approach and communicate. You want to evoke a different, better response. Eliminating toxic and inflammatory words is a powerful step in this process.

Should and shouldn't

These words remove someone's independence and autonomy to run their own life. "You should . . ." "You shouldn't have . . ." "They need to . . ." "He has to just . . ." "You ought to . . ." These are opinions that we all have a right to hold in our thoughts, but it might help our relationship if we censor them.

Try replacing a *should* with your own wish, want, or hope.

Not: "You should take that inside." Instead go with "I would love it if you would take that inside."

Not: "You shouldn't talk so loudly in here." Instead try "I would prefer it if you could speak a little quieter while we're inside." Or, "I would like it if you . . ."

Not: "You should want to call me more often." Try "I hope you can get to a place of wanting to call me more often."

Changing from "You should" to "I wish" takes the focus and energy away from the other's shortcoming and instead turns your want or need into a favor that they can do to show love. It becomes a request that your partner will most likely want to meet rather than resist.

Why

The word "why" is valuable in lots of ways. Yet when we use it to communicate our feelings about something and how it impacts us, a "why" can sound critical and even contemptuous.

"Why didn't you call me?" "Why didn't you take out the garbage like I asked?" "Why don't you just do it this way?" What the listener is really hearing underneath these questions is "Why are you such an idiot that you...?"

If you are really curious about something and need to use "why," lead with your intention and use soothing words. "I don't want to be critical here; I am just curious why you chose to do it differently than we agreed?" Can you feel the difference? When you are disappointed and say, "Why didn't you just call me?" your partner will hear, "What's wrong with you that you didn't call me?" Instead, how about "I wish you would have called me. Next time would you please do that?" While it is true that conflicts can still arise when you use these softer ways of communicating, I am confident that they will be fewer and smaller as a result. If your partner still gets defensive, they may be responding to feeling badly about disappointing you. That's a good thing in that it means they care!

Always and never

It is true that "never" and "always" are not accurate words. They are critical and tend to flood the other person with hopelessness. Beating someone up is not the best way to get them on board to meet your needs. Sure, we might say that our partner has never jumped out of a plane, but that isn't critical. It isn't a personal attack on their character. "You never do the dishes" is critical. "You always leave your socks on the floor" is critical. Remove "always" and "never" from your vocabulary and replace them with softer words that won't elicit a defensive response. How about "sometimes," "often," "frequently," or "not as much as I would like." These are probably more accurate and don't squash your partner's hope that you will be accepting of them, warts and all. Better yet, "I know you try to pick up your socks, thank you, and I wish you would do it more often." That is so much more effective and less attacking than "You never pick up your socks." Once again, what we say and how we say it matters.

But

Ever hear this? *Never put your "but" in front of an angry person.* The little word "but" is called a coordinating conjunction in the English language. However, using "but" in a relationship has the power to dismiss a whole person and their viewpoint. I hear this frequently during repair attempts between couples in my office. "I'm sorry I said that hurtful thing to you, but you started it by..." "I know you tried to help, and I appreciate that, but you always..." "I understand, but . . ." or the dreaded "Yeah, but..."

The word "but" communicates, "Forget everything I just said, what I really think and feel is . . ." It wrecks repair attempts. For example, "I am sorry you were hurt when I said that, but I am angry at you." See how it dismisses or minimizes the apology? It says, "I'm really not sorry." It hijacks the repair and brings the focus on the speaker's experience, hurt, or need.

It will feel weird at first. However, the best word to use instead is the word "and." "I'm sorry you were hurt when I said that, AND I am still angry at you." The word "and" allows the first part, the apology and its validation, to stick while allowing the speaker an opportunity to share what is true for them.

Step 4

Experiment for This Step

Get inflammatory words out of your vocabulary and out of your relationship. Eliminate "should" and "shouldn't," "why," "always," "never," and "but."

Each week pick one word to eliminate from your communication. Post a note with the word and a line through it in a few places you frequent to keep you mindful of the goal. Model the emotional safety you want in return from your partner.

Work on eliminating hurtful words

Start with the word "should." Post it on a sticky on your monitor, on your dashboard, in the bathroom. Notice how often you think and feel the word "should" and how you communicate your thoughts and needs around it. Try to replace it with "I wish . . ." or "I would have liked . . ." and see what the response from the other is.

Next week move on to the word "why," then "always" and "never" and finally "but." Express your need or want without using these words.

I think you will see how this will help start to disarm the other person instead of seeing them raise their defensive shields. Play a game with yourself. See how long you can go without speaking each of these words. The goal is to avoid leaving your partner feeling *should-on*, judged as not worthy, and criticized.

Help your partner clean up their vocabulary

This involves gentle, very gentle, feedback. If your partner *shoulds* on you or uses some of the hurtful words we discussed in this chapter, you will want to help them start to see the impact on you.

When they are talking and use one of these forbidden words, don't interrupt them! Wait for your natural time to respond, state your intention, and be gentle.

"Honey, I want to listen to what you are saying and want to help. First, though, can I let you know that when you tell me 'I should do that,' I start to feel hurt and defensive inside; I start to shut down. Can you work on *asking* me instead?"

"Babe, I appreciate what you're saying and want to talk about that with you. First, I need to let you know that when you say, 'You never take out the garbage,' I don't feel appreciated. I get hurt and then find it hard to hear what you are saying."

You can also bring this up later if you do not believe they can tolerate the quick break from the conversation. Let them know you are specifically working on eliminating words that might be hurtful for them and invite them to join you. Wouldn't that be great!

Now that you've worked to get some of the divisive words out of your vocabulary, let's work on getting rid of some weapons out of your relationship.

Chapter Ten

Step 5
Stop the Guerilla Warfare

Guerrilla warfare is when a small group of combat-ants use tactics such as an ambush, hit-and-run, and sabotage to fight. If you want a happy, romantic, and secure relationship, ambushes, sabotage, and hit-and-run tactics won't get you there.

As a professional I can honestly say that it is generally not a good idea to terrorize your partner. At least, not if you want to have a safe, nurturing, and loving relationship. Communicating your needs and emotions through an ambush or hit-and-run strategy is devastating to your relationships because it removes emotional safety. Emotional safety is the freedom to open up and be vulnerable, to give yourself to the relationship. You can't do that if you are busy looking over your shoulder, waiting to get stabbed in the back.

Having a set of *rules of engagement* that you both honor is part of what creates emotional safety. Rules of engagement define what's okay and what's not. In the movie *Top Gun* (*TOP GUN*. Paramount, 1986), there is a scene where Maverick is getting chewed out for buzzing the tower in his jet. The commander says, "Top Gun rules of engagement exist for your safety and for that of your team. They are not flexible, nor am I."

In your relationship, it is no different. There are simply some things you just DO NOT do for everyone's safety, period. You are *in* the relationship; you are half *of* the relationship. You must do your part to protect it from the deep wounds that guerilla warfare can inflict. Couples create these rules, often without realizing it. Early in the relationship when you have fights that grow in volatility, you are slowly making it okay by staying. You are inadvertently communicating, *Even though you treat me this way, I will stay.* Truthfully, if the relationship is too painful, eventually someone *will* leave. The idea that marriage is forever is romantic and even admirable, but divorce rates don't validate that belief. Marriage is a choice because you willfully give up freedom to be in the relationship. When it hurts enough, you'll take back your freedom.

Simply against the rules

In the last chapter we talked about criticism which could easily fit into this chapter too. However, while criticism is often direct, the weapons of guerilla war are often more subtly delivered. In this chapter we are focusing on:

- o   Contempt
- o   Defensiveness
- o   Sarcasm
- o   Blame

Ideally you will work with your partner to install boundaries, or rules of engagement, to keep these hurtful things out of

117

your relationship. If you want to maintain the emotional safety to talk, share, love, and be intimate, you have to work to make sure you both can be vulnerable with each other. This means no drive-by shootings and no ambush attacks. If you do, you better break out the repair kit.

Let's dissect these four weapons so you can start working on getting them out of your relationship.

Contempt

One of the definitions of the word *contempt* includes disgust. Does it ever feel as though your partner is communicating this to you? Say the following out loud: "You disgust me."

Let that soak into your mind and body for a moment. *You disgust me.* Have you ever felt that from your partner? When your partner communicates this, you may also feel them saying, *You are worthless.* What an awful feeling to have! *You are disgusting and worthless.* I bet you don't feel like being cuddly after that.

Contempt can come out in subtle ways. When we are talking about something important and our partner rolls their eyes or looks away, that is contempt. When they come home and do not say "hello," that is contempt. It's like they are saying, *You do not exist.*

When they pretend to listen, but are looking at their phone and texting someone else, that is contempt. When your partner says things under their breath, this is contempt. Other examples of contempt include personal insults, mocking, finger-pointing, or putting a hand up while you are talking.

Contempt can also come out in more volatile ways. Name-calling, with or without colorful adult adjectives, is a common way this happens. Yelling and screaming make it all worse. So do put-downs, shutting the door in someone's face, or hanging up in anger. It is also contemptuous to be looking at an electronic screen or turning your back and walking away while they're talking. These all hurt. They also violate the rules of engagement for a healthy, happy, loving relationship because they communicate disgust or worthlessness. Sadly, this stuff happens in many relationships. We humans are just mean to each other sometimes.

Sarcasm

Another type of "hit-and-run" attack is sarcasm. What's subtle about sarcasm is that it comes disguised as a compliment, but it is really an underhanded insult. "You're really great at that, aren't you?" This would be a sarcastic put-down if it came after you had made a mistake.

The fact that it has a whisper of truth can make it painful, too. For instance, when walking to the back of a very long line at the coffee shop, you quip to yourself, "So glad I slept in." You are really saying you regret sleeping in, which may be true. In this case it isn't directed at anyone other than yourself. No harm, no foul, though you did just put yourself down.

Where it gets to be a problem is when it is directed at your partner. In the same scenario, imagine your partner slept too long, contributing to you both being late. While walking to the back of the long line with them you say, "So glad you slept in." Ouch! Can you feel the attack? The criticism? The disgust? The contempt? Don't be surprised if you find yourself buying your own coffee and sitting alone.

Sarcasm in relationships is a problem because the comments are sneaky jabs in the back. They are harsh or critical comments wrapped in apparent humor. Yet, sarcasm masks the real emotion and need: "I wish you hadn't slept in this morning. I don't like being late."

Sarcasm is really just a snotty remark, often pointing out someone's shortcoming. "Well, that's really helpful" or "Oh, you're so brilliant," said in reply to someone who just tripped on something, will be hurtful, not funny.

If your partner uses sarcasm, just like all reactions, they are really doing two things. Firstly, they are reacting to an emotion versus expressing that emotion and the need underneath it. Remember, the reaction will get them the opposite of what they want. Secondly they are belittling you, which will also get them the opposite of what they want. Insane, isn't it?

Why do people use sarcasm? On the surface it seems like a less confrontational way to express emotions and needs. However, oftentimes it is how a family communicates and it becomes a habit. Perhaps it is you, rather than your partner, who uses sarcasm, or perhaps it's both of you. Either way, it is time to stop. Be direct with what you feel and need, and life will be easier.

Defensiveness

Being defensive is an understandable and natural response to feeling attacked or criticized. Defensiveness is a way of shifting responsibility, often when we are feeling blamed. It can be explaining what happened or justifying an action or decision. When you approach your partner with an issue or hurt and they become defensive, most likely you will feel dismissed. Instead of validating your experience or feelings, it seems as though they are explaining why you *shouldn't* feel the way you do and why your needs are not important.

If you and your partner play the blame game a lot, you may

find yourself on alert. You have to be ready to defend, explain, or justify your behavior *or else*. You want to get off the hook from the crummy feelings that blame creates. It sucks to feel wrong, not good enough, not accepted, or seen as having evil intentions all the time. Guess what, your partner is no different. They don't like this either!

Defensiveness can also be when you reply to someone's feedback or criticism with one of your own. Suppose your partner says, "Why didn't you call me today?" If you answer, "Why didn't you call ME?" they will experience this as a defensive move and become frustrated because you've just flipped it around on them. Now they'll have to try and flip it back on you—the blame game is on! There is actually a highly scientific and technical term for this. It's called "tit for tat." Partners in relationships suffering from tit for tat find that everything sets off a fight that never ends up in repair because you both are too hurt.

The problem with your partner becoming defensive is that you instinctively know they have shut down and are no longer listening to you. They are no longer open and responsive to your needs because they are busy defending their words or actions instead of listening to what's important to you. The odds that this interaction will lead to an understanding or the change you wanted are low.

Blame

You are responsible for your own behavior. No one *makes* you do anything. Sure, there is always a chain of events that are cause and effect. Yet, just because your partner accused you of being critical of them doesn't mean you have to defend yourself by pointing out how they were critical of you yesterday.

Blame is an offensive way to defend yourself. It is going on

121

the attack instead of explaining. It is the "tit for tat" and like the other weapons we've just discussed, less than helpful.

What blame often does is start the *content spreading* that will escalate your conversation. You talk about being hurt over something that was said. In response, your partner gets defensive by bringing up what you did yesterday. To defend that, you bring up what they did last week. Next your partner ups the ante by accusing you of *always* doing something. You raise it even more by saying how they *never* do something. Soon you're both listing every relationship problem and hurt you can think of, and nothing gets resolved.

Resentment

Why do you or your partner express these things to the other? Sometimes it is because of resentment. Resentment is a highly toxic poison that will kill your relationship if it isn't released. It starts when you experience the bitterness of feeling unfairly treated. To fight this, as you have learned, the feelings of anger flow working to set boundaries and create changes. The goal is to get back on the same page with your partner. Over time as you work to repair the issue and renegotiate back to fairness, the thoughts and feelings of anger will mostly subside. Phew.

However, if what happened that left you feeling bitter also included a sense of betrayal, which is a breaking of trust, then your heart will harden. Now it feels as though you cannot trust your partner like before the betrayal. You can probably imagine how this could come about through something such as infidelity. However it can also happen over time when your partner is not responsive to you. You signed up for a partnership, for them to be there for you. If they are not, over time, the trust you had will break and resentment will fill the cracks.

Let's say your partner gambled away their paycheck, of course without asking you first. Understandably you will see this as a betrayal of trust and feel angry. Since you are hurt, angry and don't trust them now, your brain will start working to solve the problem so you can feel better. Unfortunately this is where the problem is because no choice seems to lead to happiness. Part of you may want to leave the relationship because *I don't deserve to be treated this way*. Part of you probably wants to kick them out because you want them to hurt. Part of you doesn't want to leave because of commitment. Still another part of you doesn't want to act in a way that is retaliatory because that's not who you are. You're stuck and being pulled by all these choices and parts!

Since there is no choice that leads to escape from the pain associated with the issue; no choice seems to lead to happiness, you are trapped. Happiness is no longer an option. You are stuck in an intolerable situation which is a form of depression. One of the characteristics of depression is that it saps all your motivation to do things that might feel good. Your brain, in an act of self-protection from more hurt, freezes you and drains your motivation. You don't want to move toward, be intimate or engage with your partner. The bitterness from feeling unfairly treated and reminders of the betrayal constantly flow in your brain. It won't let go!

When you feel betrayed or unfairly treated, when you feel trapped in your own choices you will keep experiencing the pain. You will re-experience the unfairness of being on the painful receiving end of what your partner did and remain bitter about the injustice you involuntarily have to swallow. It is as though your partner fed you poison. What does it feel like you want now? You want them to suffer and hurt too! Your behavior may turn passive aggressive or your may become distant. You want them to see you are hurt and you want them to respond. This is when we become prickly to be around through sarcasm and criticism, or easily defensive and blaming in return.

Dealing with Resentment

I have found that there are a few ways to deal with resentment; a couple for you to work through alone and one to work out with your partner. Which one is best depends on the state of your relationship and your partner's ability to understand, have compassion and own their part.

If you have to go it alone, one way to work on resentment is to decide to set boundaries. You may need to make changes to the rules of your relationship or even changes to how your life is managed. Figure out what you need to feel better and then go to your partner and ask for what you need. Perhaps you need to take over all the finances, but to make it fair they have to agree to take over all the housework. This new agreement can feel like there is a *making of amends* piece along with changes that help you feel like new boundaries are in place. That's critical to re-building trust.

Another step in working on resentment on your own is to take your power back. When you accept a situation because you *choose* to in some way, you can feel better about the situation. Make a decision by finishing the following sentence:

"I choose to _____, because _____."

"I choose to stay in this relationship because I still love my partner." If you don't like your job and feel resentful for feeling trapped, you might say, "I choose to work here because I want

124

the paycheck it brings." Now you are making an empowered choice. Own that choice and don't blame your partner for that.

The best way though, at least in my view, is to be able to express your hurt and upset-ness with your partner. When you feel understood, when they can own their part, you are not alone with your feelings. However, this is tricky because if they become defensive, dismissive, blaming or move into their own guilt and shame, you won't leave the conversation feeling understood. The ability to be compassionate with each other and take ownership for one's contribution are key attributes of a strong relationship.

Resentment, more than anything else, has the toxic potential to unwind your relationship because it blocks partners from moving toward each other to repair deep hurts. Many couples who come into counseling find they waited too long. Don't let this be you! If you or your partner are resentful and can't work through it alone, find a good counselor to help. Working through this stuff can be hard, yet it is critical to your relationship's long term health, happiness and security.

How to holster the weapons

If you are the partner who is using these guerilla weapons, contempt, sarcasm, defensiveness and blame, remember, the silver bullet in relationships is always mindfulness. When you can be mindful of how you feel and what you need, you can choose to respond thoughtfully instead of simply reacting from your emotions. This may mean you have to work on noticing your emotions and your thoughts. In a moment when you feel hurt, do you need to be appreciated? Accepted? Understood? Important? Close? Or, to have your partner reflect that you are a good person? Do you need validation or empathy?

When you feel that urge to react in your body, try to stay *cu-*

125

rious instead. This is a thinking and reasoning brain function that can interrupt the fight-or-flight response that compels you to say something mean.

When you do not default to saying or doing something hurtful, you lower the odds your partner will do or say something hurtful in return. A different response from you evokes a different response from your partner, and this changes how the relationship feels.

Let's say that you are late picking your partner up. When they get into the car, instead of a happy greeting they give you a dirty look. You could get defensive with "I couldn't help it; traffic was bad!" Or, be compassionate and curious. "I'm so sorry I am late. I hope you didn't have to stand there too long." In my experience it is hard for someone to stay reactive when you are being soft and apologetic.

If your partner is the reactive one, you can still stay in a calm and curious place. If your partner jabs you with a sarcastic comment and hurts your feelings, remember that no one *makes* you retaliate. If you can stay curious and see them as hurt and needing something they cannot express, you can avoid getting sucked into that negative cycle. Maybe you can even help them feel better. So remember, you don't have to accept every invitation for a fight.

Just because they said something mean doesn't mean you have to retaliate. If you can stay curious, you have a better chance of offering a caring and compassionate response to their underlying need. This will help you change the moment toward a better direction.

Staying curious might look like "Whoa, hey, I'm sorry if I said something that upset or hurt you. I don't want to hurt you. Is there something you need?" Or, "I'm sorry, I didn't mean for you to feel defensive. What are you wanting here?" Or, "Ouch, that hurt. Did I do something to upset you?" If your partner has expressed contempt or sarcasm or become defensive, to help change the cycle and evoke a different response from your partner, be curious about them, what they are feeling, and what they might need. Don't get sucked into the negative cycle.

If you do these things to your partner

Don't. The behaviors I have just described in this chapter are hurtful, mean and relationship killing behaviors. They remove the emotional safety by communicating, if *I am hurt or upset, I will turn on you and attack.* You might not be intending to say that to your partner, but I promise that's what they are hearing. It is up to you to stop sending that message, even if your partner sending it to you.

Sometimes all the thoughts and judgments in your head just pop out. Maybe they are remnants from how it was in your family growing up, or perhaps over time you have become more hurt and upset in your relationship. Either way, *you are always responsible for your own behavior.* For you to bring a healthy and loving contribution to your relationship, you must not give in to the reactionary impulses, the fight or flight responses that your emotions spur. If you can't do that, you might consider seeking out a counselor to help you work on your emotional regulation.

Being more mindful of your thoughts and feelings is a step toward getting a handle on reactivity. You have to be aware of the rising tide to do something about it. Otherwise you'll just start drowning and flip into survival mode. The next step that might be helpful is to keep your mouth closed so words don't squirt out. You will find that if you do keep your mouth closed and just breathe for a count of ten, that urge to react will flow through you and pass. You may also need to tell your partner, "I'm upset right now and cannot engage nicely. I am going to go in the other room for twenty minutes. I promise to talk about this after that." That would be managing yourself and your emotions and protecting your partner and your relationship.

If your partner does these to you

So what if they are doing these things to you? The same rules apply as above. You are still responsible for your behavior. Just because they are upset and are attacking, doesn't mean you have to retaliate. Don't accept that invitation! Instead, train your partner to treat you better. Stay patient and calm. If you need to withdraw for a short time, say so. Just be sure to say you'll be back.

If early in a discussion they jab you with one of the weapons in this chapter, you can start with the, "that's not helpful right now." Later you can circle back to work on repair. Talk about how the conversation went, what hurt and what you need to be different. If the hurtful behavior continues you can move to this. "I know you are feeling hurt right now, AND saying those things is not okay. I am going to go into the other room for twenty minutes and will be willing to try talking again after that."

When you return, do not spend time talking about who said what. If you have to go there, acknowledge that it is possible you have it wrong. That will help your partner feel less of a need to be defensive. Work to own your own contribution and follow the repair model we talked about in Step one. This includes asking your partner to own something that hurt you.

Boundaries are important to set. You do not want train your

partner that it is okay to treat you in ways described in this chapter. You never want to punish or retaliate by leaving as that will backfire. This is about setting a boundary for how you will allow yourself to be treated. If you do step away you must tell them when you are returning to talk and you have to make sure you follow through. Otherwise they will not trust you.

Step 5

Experiment for This Step

I'm not sure if curiosity killed a cat, but I do believe it can put a stop to the weapons of guerilla warfare. When you are hurting inside, you want someone to care enough to ask. In this step I want you to focus on the idea of being curious when interacting with your partner. Try to get them to open up about what's going on inside with their thoughts and feelings. Or, if they won't go there, try to find out what they believe they need.

This might not solve the issue, but hopefully it will get you out of the cycle of guerilla warfare that derails your efforts to solve the problem. Even better, maybe it will get you into conversations that can lead to a better connection.

Stop attacking your partner

If you find yourself expressing your feelings through actions of contempt, using sarcasm, or being defensive and blaming, don't. Seriously, just don't. It is never okay. Instead, it's time to get in touch with your deeper needs. If you feel that urge coming on, just stop and ask yourself, *What do I really need right now?*

If things get heated, you can tell your partner, "I really need to take a break from this conversation. I will be back in thirty minutes and will talk more then." If you say this, *you must return!* Whatever happens, don't let yourself become flooded with emotions and don't let the issue escalate. Express your needs or take a break. A break can give you time to calm down and actually figure out what you need. Then come back and express what you need in a way they can hear. You will probably have to do some listening too, as well as repair anything that was hurtful. Be prepared to own your side of what happened.

Help your partner curb their attacks

If your partner communicates using some of the hurtful weapons in this chapter, there is a way to manage this. When they do something or say something hurtful, simply say in response, "That's not helpful right now." Then be curious, which would be something like "You sound as though you need something right now."

If your partner starts playing the blame game with "You do it too," try offering, "If I do, I'm sorry. I will stop."

If the conversation escalates, you can always do what I suggested above and wave the white flag. "We're not doing well right now. Can we come back and talk in thirty minutes?" Or an hour, or whatever you need.

Part 3
The Recipe for Love

You've heard of the Golden Rule, right? Treat other people like you want to be treated. How about stepping up to the Platinum Rule: treat your partner like they want to be treated.

Chapter Eleven

Step 6
Make Time to Connect

*Couples build their love through the intimacy of con-
versation. Then when life happens, they get busy and
abandon what worked. If you want to rebuild love and
connection, do what worked in the first place: talk to
each other again!*

There are two types of silence I want to address in this chapter. One is the regular "we never talk" silence, the other is
the "I'm upset with you and don't want to talk to you" silence.
Let's start with the kind caused by angry feelings such as resentment that make you want to avoid talking to your partner.

When you are arguing, it isn't always easy to keep interacting with your partner calmly. When things escalate some need a
little distance to calm down before reengaging. Emotions are
chemicals that flood your body to get you to act. During the fight
and even for a while after the fight is over, especially if it didn't
get resolved, those chemicals are still lingering and take time to
dissipate. Some of us can do this quickly, and some not so quickly. A little distance can be helpful for calming down before re-

pairing hurts and resuming the conversation.

Ideally you'll both talk about creating this plan in advance. Agree on the rule that if one of you has to disengage, they must say they are coming back and when. Agree to continue talking about the issue at that appointed time. That way if distance is what you or your partner needs you will be able to collaborate to make it happen with grace. In your relationship, always work to express care for the other and never completely withdraw from the relationship. "I'm still mad at you, but I'll be okay in a while. I do love you; I just need some time to calm down." That is music to the ears of those who tend to have deep anxieties about being abandoned. It is reassurance that "we're going to be okay". Statements of security express care for your partner in the midst of disconnection.

If you or your partner disengages and you end up ignoring each other, once again remember that your behaviors are a reaction to your emotions and something you will probably have to apologize for later. Ignoring someone is an expression of contempt that could say either: *You don't exist, You are worthless,* or even *You disgust me.* The sooner one of you can approach the other to try and repair the relationship, the better. Research shows that once we get psychologically aroused into the fight-or-flight brain, we need twenty to thirty minutes to calm down, not three days. Three days is contemptuous behavior that adds to the hurt.

The common "silence"

What I really intend to get to in this chapter has more to do with basic engagement with each other as a couple. Do you talk and check in with each other during the morning routine? Or do you just go through the list of chores for the day? Is there any moment of connection during the day? What about when you are both together again in the evening? Is that more logistics and tasks, or do you make time to talk about your relationship and each other? How about before bed?

If you are not talking and sharing your life every day, if you are not keeping your partner abreast of how your daily life is going, you will start to feel disconnected.

When a new couple comes into my office to get help with their communication, one of the questions I always ask them is "When do you get together and talk?" Many times they look back at me blankly, like I asked if they speak Martian. Finally, one will say, "We don't."

Sitting down and talking to your partner is Relationship 101 stuff. How else can you stay in touch with each other and keep up on each other's hopes, dreams, worries, fears, and lives? When else do you give each other feedback and fine-tune your relationship? How else do you maintain the connection? No one wants to hold hands and have sex with someone who won't talk and share their thoughts and feelings. Ironically when couples first become close, they prioritize being with each other, talk for hours about everything under the sun, and as a result, feel close. Have you ever heard or said, "We used to talk for hours about nothing. I didn't want to hang up the phone at night." Then it all goes away in the midst of life happening. The ability to talk and share is lost because it isn't a priority anymore.

If you have children, taking ten minutes to check in with your partner is excellent modeling. When the children see you taking time to speak and listen as you reconnect with your partner for these ten minutes, it will serve them well. Don't let your children sit between you during these ten minutes.

In working to teach them patience while you prioritize your relationship, you are teaching your children impulse and self-control. You are also reassuring that their world is secure. Focus on your partner for those ten minutes to communicate that they are important to you.

Create moments to feel connected

So how do you create connection? My belief is that those six attachment needs we keep talking about must be flowing back and forth for two people to feel connected. Information that says, "You are important to me. I appreciate you. I accept you. I understand you. I want to be close to you. I think you are a good and lovable person."

When we conduct our lives in a way that considers how we impact our partner and endeavor to communicate those six attachment needs to them, most likely we will have a safe and loving relationship.

When you leave in the morning for work or whatever you do, and are gone for eight to ten hours, you and your partner will have lived a whole day apart. You'll have seen people, places, and things. You've had experiences and emotions and learned new things. You might think your day is the same old humdrum as yesterday, but since your partner wasn't there with you, they don't know this and don't share that thought. Your partner doesn't know what your life has been like while away from them. They need to. When you go out into the world, experience new things, and have adventures, you return hoping to share these with your partner. If he or she does not ask about your day, your life, they communicate that they do not care. When you ask your partner, "How was your day?" and the answer consists of "Fine," don't you feel cheated? They are not sharing what's in their head.

136

They are closed and keeping you out. The connection dims in this moment.

The magic of talking

Talking with your partner can bridge the distance between you. Spending time recounting your day helps each of you understand what life is like for each other. It is an opportunity for empathy and compassion, which communicates, *I care.*

Can you guess what many couples who are struggling to communicate don't do? That's right; they don't prioritize a time together to talk.

Since we all have busy lives, it is important to refresh your knowledge about your partner every day. Talking together is the best way to do this. When couples say, "We don't communicate," what they are really saying is "We don't understand each other." I would say, of course not. You aren't talking!

When couples don't talk about the little daily things, most likely they are not repairing the hurts along the way either. Couples who don't talk about what they think, feel, and want in life stop sharing their dreams. That's a lonely place. To cope, they may begin dreaming about being without their partner or with someone else. This is one of the ways partners grow apart. All because you stop talking to each other.

Time to end the silence

To change all this, you may need to invite your partner into a conversation. "Hey, I haven't talked to you all day. Can we sit for a few minutes and check in with each other?"

If not, ask when. If they show up but do not share, be okay with that for now.

Model sharing and also be curious and inquire about them in specific ways. "Did anything funny happen today?" This can direct their mind to something specific and is much better than "How was your day?" Also consider asking about a specific person, place, or thing you know was part of their day.

This time together has to be a priority, even above the kids. If you do this after work, or before or right after dinner, let the kids know this is your couple time and they need to play quietly. In doing this you are communicating to them that their life is stable and secure, because their parents' relationship is secure. Don't underestimate the value of this.

Step 6

Experiment for This Step

Establish a regular routine of time(s) when you can and do talk with your partner every day. Talk about things that support the relationship and help you feel close.

Let your partner know you would like to spend a little time talking and checking in with them every day. Invite them. Don't make a big deal about a meeting. Just convey that you would like to find a ten- or twenty-minute segment that works and that this is about prioritizing your time together.

Waking-up time is a good time if you can make it work. If you try for the afternoon, don't do it over the phone, as you can't see each other's expressions and emotions. Talking while doing an activity together such as cleaning or chores can work, but only if both partners feel it is helpful to connect. After work is also a great time.

Sit on the couch together and check in; include a hug! After the kids go to bed or before your own bedtime can work too, but be careful at nighttime. Often one of you will get sleepy and leave the other feeling rejected. It is best to choose a time when you're both awake.

When's the last time you took a bath together? When is the last time you sat at the kitchen table or on the couch *without* the TV on and just talked?

End the silence

Invite your partner to share their day, every day. Ideally you would sit on the couch together (no electronics at all, TV included!) and talk about your day. Each of you tells the other person something about your day, preferably not about the other, that made you mad (irritated, annoyed, frustrated), sad (bummed, alone, left out), scared (worried, stressed, anxious), and glad (happy, excited, surprised in a good way). As the listener, be validating and empathetic. Convey interest by being curious; ask follow-up questions, *even if you are not interested.*

Work to keep your speaking time fairly short and simple. Pay attention to any cues from them that suggest they are not interested. Try to stay calm if that happens. You are trying to change the communication dynamics in your relationship. It will take time and consistency. If you do play the listener role, work to listen with curiosity, not to fix, give (unwanted) advice, or sit waiting to jump in with an opinion.

Help your partner end the silence

Since you can't control your partner, your job is to make requests and offer invitations. Getting them to approach you and initiate conversation might be too much to expect at first. Focus first on modeling what you want—talk about your experiences in a positive way while acknowledging their participation. This can help them learn to initiate. If this experience feels good, they will want more.

Then after a few weeks of initiating these moments of connection, float the idea to your partner that you would like them to initiate one of these conversations. Set them up for success by actually letting them know what you would like.

"Hey, we haven't sat and talked since Monday. I would love it if you took the initiative and invited me to sit on the couch with you and talk." You are letting them know that you want

Chapter Twelve

Step 7
Communicate You Care

*Any job done well will benefit from using the right
tool. When your partner approaches to you to share
what they are thinking and feeling, they need you to be
there for them. <u>Your partner doesn't want you to fix
anything</u>; they need to know you care. The "fix it" tool
is the wrong tool. The empathy and validation tool is
the right tool. Expressing empathy and validating is
THE fix.*

When you go to your partner and bring up something important, do they change the subject? Maybe they interrupt
you before you finish and quickly tell you what to do or say to fix
it. Even worse, do they find a way to criticize you?

If this is happening, you are going to have a hurt feeling.
You may start to believe that your partner doesn't think you are
capable, doesn't value your efforts, or doesn't understand what is
important to you. If this happens, eventually you are going to
wonder if they care about you at all. Hopefully deep down you
can hold onto the idea that they do care. If so, bravo! Yet, do you

keep experiencing moments that communicate something different? When you do not *feel* cared for, it will become hard to hold onto that belief. It will also be hard to hold onto happiness. The stress that results from that icky sensation of not feeling as though you matter is real. At a deep level there are chemicals in your body creating that chronic discomfort. Those chemicals flowing through your body will eventually impact your physical health.

Having the belief and sense that your partner cares for you is calming to your brain, body, and emotions. The feelings that flow from the belief that we matter are good ones. They are healing and soothing chemicals that our bodies need. Creating this feeling is so important that it gets its own step. So yes, I have a tool to help create this feeling. A key way to communicate that you care is done through the power of empathy and validation.

What empathy *is*

The short version of empathy is when you actually feel or can imagine feeling a small bit of what your partner feels inside. Then, with your facial expression, your touch, your tone, your words, convey this to them.

"I can see this really hurts you." Said with a compassionate face.

"I know this is so hard for you to face." Said while reaching out to hold the other person.

"It makes sense to me that you are upset." Said with a stern, *I'm joining with you on being upset* face.

"Oh, geeze. I know you hate that." Said with a face of sadness.

"That's nuts! I can't believe they said that to you." Said with an, *I'm going to defend you* tone.

Empathy and compassion can also be conveyed by reaching out and holding your partner's hand. This expresses that you see their need for comfort and that you are available to them. Can you feel how those words of empathy and the action of reaching out create connection with your partner? Would it with you?

Empathy soothes distressed emotions. Empathy mops up the painful emotions of the fight-or-flight response. On the other hand, sympathy is acknowledging the other person's experience from the outside. It's having compassion but not feeling what they might be feeling. Sympathy is about agreeing with someone's experience or feelings. Empathy is about sharing them. Sympathy isn't a bad thing. The problem is that sympathy is less personal, less intimate, less caring and more intellectual.

Sympathy looks like:

- o "I bet you don't like that."
- o "Yes, that is difficult, isn't it?"
- o "I agree that this is hard work."
- o "We are on the same page here."

Empathy is learned

Empathy is a learned skill. If, as we grow up, the people around us are empathetic to us, our brain's mirror neurons pick up the expression of emotion in the other and we grow the ability to do this for others as well. However, if this doesn't happen very much while growing up, we fail to develop this ability. It can, however, be learned. Our brains can change. We can learn and grow. So if your partner is not very empathetic or if perhaps you aren't, this dynamic *can* be changed.

To help my clients start to understand empathy, I like to of-

144

fer the analogy of us each having an emotional swimming pool. Instead of water imagine this pool is filled with your own thoughts and feelings that you swim around in. For you to be empathetic to your partner, you have to get out of your own pool for a moment and jump into their pool. Imagine swimming around in your partner's experience. You would think, *Gee, is that what it's like to be you? Oh man, this sucks!* Having imagined what they might be feeling, you are bable to express that you "get it" using words of empathy.

When you do, it will sound like this:

- o "Oh wow, this really hurts!"
- o "That's awful to be treated that way."
- o "This really sucks! You worked so hard to avoid this."
- o "This is incredibly sad right now."
- o "I don't blame you for being angry about this."
- o "I'm starting to see how worried you are about that."

Each of these statements expresses care and concern. They say to your partner, *I have compassion for you in this moment. I am here with you. You are not alone in feeling this way.*

Empathy is the bridge that you build with your partner to stay close when they are in distress. Empathy says, *I believe you have a right to feel this way.* Most importantly, empathy will go in and soothe the emotional fight-or-flight urge that your partner is feeling and often keep them from escalating. When you lead with empathy, your partner will *feel felt.* If you lead with a "fix it" suggestion, or a critical comment, they will get angry with you because skipping over their emotions and problem solving communicates, *You are incompetent and I need to fix you.*

Empathy can help mop up the feelings of fight or flight be-

145

cause if they get empathy, they are not alone in the world. Empathy helps them feel seen and felt. Being understood is an attachment need, so do not underestimate the value of leading with an empathetic response.

You can learn empathy

When I was consciously learning how to be better at empathy, I would go to the grocery store and engage the checker with a simple question. Depending on the time of day, morning, afternoon, or evening, I would say, "Looks like you have the early bird shift." Or, "Looks like you have the late shift." I was simply making a nonjudgmental observation, fishing for any emotion to which I could offer empathy.

They would express their thoughts and feelings in response, often with a facial expression to match. "Yeah, I had an early one today. It'll be a long day." My response might be, "Oh geeze, long days at work are the pits." Which is my effort to communicate I understand what it's like for them. Or, "I have to work until midnight, but I don't mind because I like my job." I might reply with, "Oh, that does make it easier."

If I can learn it, you can learn empathy too and so can your partner. People change in therapy all the time; it's possible!

Intentionally looking for moments to be empathetic means tuning in to your partner's emotions and moving toward them in that moment with an expression of compassion. Interestingly, you can express empathy with a gesture. When you see them in distress, give them a hug, if you're sitting with them, touch their knee or reach out to hold their hand.

These are empathetic gestures that say, *I care that this is hard, and I am here. You are not alone.*

Does empathy mean I agree?

I want to note that being empathetic does not mean you agree with *why* your partner feels the way they feel. It is simply communicating, *I understand you. I see your emotions and want you to know I am here for you.* Sometimes I will be asked, "How can I be empathetic if I don't agree that they should feel upset right now?" Yes, that is hard for many of us. It means putting aside our own thoughts and feelings (judgment) and being available to support our partner. Just because you might not believe they *should* feel that way doesn't mean they don't.

Maintaining emotional safety is critical. You want your partner to feel the *I have your back because you matter to me* sense. This means communicating you will be there when life is hard for them. The relationship will suffer if you communicate that; *I will be there for you if and when I deem your emotions appropriate and reasonable.* You communicate your care and concern through empathetic responsiveness to each other's experiences. I believe this is one of the markers of a successful relationship.

Empathy shattered

Where this goes wrong and causes your partner to wince is when you do not jump into their pool and instead stay in your own. This happens when you offer unwanted advice in an effort to fix things.

In that moment you may see your partner in distress and find it hard *for you.* Naturally you don't want your partner to be unhappy, so of course you want to fix them. If you fix things, it will be better for you both.

Naturally when my wife is sad, I want to fix it. If I do the

147

laundry and shrink her favorite sweater, naturally I want to fix it and buy her a new one. Then she won't be sad, right? When she expresses her frustration with me I will blow it if I say, "Just go buy another one." I can even mess the moment up worse by adding some dismissiveness such as "It's no big deal, it's just a sweater." Still worse, I could become critical with "You're too sensitive."

Instead, I would do much better, and you will too, by offering a little repair and compassion, some empathy! How about "Sweetheart, I'm sorry I shrunk your shirt; I know that was one you liked." If I express this empathy and compassion for how my wife feels, I will be offering some comfort for her hurt feelings. This response will help her build trust that I am able to *be with her* when she is hurting.

Only then can I take out the fix-it tool. In this case the final step is for me to make amends with "Let me take you shopping for a new one."

Validation is helpful too

Validation and empathy are sort of similar. I would say they are kissing cousins. Validation is an important and powerful tool to have in your relationship toolbox. It sounds and feels like a compliment, like acknowledgment.

o   "Hey, that dress looks great on you."
o   "Yes, that's an important point you made."
o   "You really do work hard."

Validation is acknowledgment that communicates; *I think you make good choices.* It also can express the idea *I think you are a good and competent person,* which is the "reflect the good in

148

me" attachment need. Validating others is a good habit to have if you ever interact and connect with other human beings. In fact, did you know there is a mathematical formula for connection?

Connection = Validation + Empathy

Becoming a more validating and empathetic person will absolutely make a difference in your relationships. I hope you will work hard to add this to your relationship tool box.

Two words to avoid: "I understand . . ."

A strange thing sometimes happens when couples are working to learn how to empathize with and validate each other. I ask one partner to turn toward the other and offer empathy or validation. They turn and say, "I understand how you feel." But sometimes their partner immediately says, "No, you don't understand." Their partner is right.

No one can fully understand another's experience. That's why it works best to say, "I am starting to understand." Or, "I am starting to see how much this hurts you." That small change makes a monumental difference.

Emotional regulation required

To be empathetic, both you and your partner must learn to manage your emotions and curb your reactions. Being empathetic requires that you be in your thinking and reasoning brain, not your lizard brain, which quickly moves into fight or flight, or that reactionary state that makes things worse.

Imagine a child who has just touched the stove and burned

her finger. Since she is little and has never experienced this before, she is probably crying loudly. Of course, it hurts! Now she is unsure of what to do. If the parent shows up with a scared or angry look on his face and starts yelling at the child, would you imagine this would go better or worse for her? If the parent cannot stay in their thinking and reasoning brain and instead flips into a reactionary fight-or-flight mode, everyone's emotional state will spiral out of control. If this happens chaos will reign in that moment.

As an adult you might be clear about not touching the stove, yet life tosses many other things that burn and hurt. The stress and pressure from life and all the painful experiences probably cause you to be emotional at times. What happens when you make a mistake and your partner loses control of their emotions? What happens when you come home after losing your job and instead of being consoled, are you chewed out? Can you see how emotional safety goes out the window? When your partner is able to stay with you, when they know how to calm and soothe your emotions, you feel better. When you trust them to be there for you, the bond between you grows stronger. Do you know how to do this for them?

Step 7

Experiment for This Step

Look for opportunities to express empathy toward your partner. When they are having an emotion, try to imagine feeling what they are feeling and convey to them that you see it and care. Be a model of empathy and compassion with your partner. Remember, fixing them means evoking a different response from them, and that means changing your input.

Be empathetic toward your partner

Anytime you are interacting with your partner and they seem to be emotional, start by acknowledging whatever experience they are having through an empathetic response. It is okay to be curious too, which helps them feel as though they matter to you. When you see your partner in need, you have a chance to try and fix it. *Don't!* That's the wrong tool. Instead, communicate some empathy and compassion to show you care. Look for these moments on purpose and offer an empathetic statement. Notice how your conversation goes more easily after that. Hopefully your modeling of this will increase the chances of you getting it back.

Be validating

There are always multiple truths. What is true for you may not be true for your partner and visa versa. Always validate their side, whether you agree or not; always acknowledge that what you see, feel, believe, know, may not be they same for them. This can prevent many a fight. Here is what it looks like:

"I know you have a different view on this, and (never "but") for me I feel this way."

"I know you see that as important and want to talk about it, and what I really need to talk about is this over here."

"I realize you have a different way you would like to approach this, and for me I would like to do it this way."

Note that using the word "and" validates their side whereas the word "but" dismisses and picks a fight.

Help your partner be empathetic toward you

You need empathy and validation too. Giving empathy to your partner is modeling what you want to get back from them, but it won't happen right away. Like most of these steps, we are planting the seeds that will take time to sprout. One way to accelerate this is to ask for an empathetic gesture. Let's say you are about to share something from your day that was difficult.

Lead with your intention and express your need. "I am hoping you can just listen for a few minutes and be on my side. I don't need you to fix anything, okay?" Or, "I would like you to acknowledge the effort I put in here."

Eventually you will want to talk about empathy and validation in your relationship. This will help in getting your partner on board with the idea of working together to add more empathy and validation and help you both feel understood and connected.

Chapter Thirteen

Step 8
Be Responsive

When you were a baby, if no one responded when you were in need, you could have died. Sometimes as adults, when someone isn't responding to us, we react as though we could still die. Rarely is this true.

The domain name for my relationship counseling website is *securelove.net*. I chose that because that is what I want to help my clients create. One day I had a client come in and ask what secure love meant to me. I thought for a moment and answered with one word: responsiveness. The idea of responsiveness and trust that your partner will respond is, I believe, the most critical component of any close relationship. So if I had to pick only one chapter for you to read and follow to create that more secure relationship, this is the one.

Responsiveness is not obedience

It is important to note that responsiveness does not mean obedience. If my wife calls out from the other room asking for my attention and help, responsiveness does not mean I have to drop everything in that instant and run to her side, though she might like that. It does not mean I have to immediately comply. That would be obedience.

"Sit, boy!" No, that would not work.

Responsiveness simply means I respond in a way that meets both our needs. "I'm sorry, sweetie. I am right in the middle of something. Can I be there in a few minutes?" That is different from ignoring her request, pretending not to hear it, or yelling back. "Stop screaming at me from across the house!" No, that won't work either.

Responsiveness is attentiveness or *attunement*. If I notice my wife is bothered by something and I respond in a way to help or protect her, I am keeping her on my radar. By doing so I am communicating, *I am paying attention to you. You matter to me.*

This allows her to feel close and safe with me, which helps her value and need me. When she communicates that she values and needs me, I feel calm and secure about the relationship. Can you see the circle? Can you see how I can contribute to getting my own needs met?

Respond with reassurance

Does your partner respond to you? Be brutally honest with yourself. Do you respond to your partner's needs effectively? Would they agree?

Remember from earlier how your brain monitors the connection between you both on a constant basis. Your brain monitors your partner's availability and accessibility.

It wants to make sure your partner is going to respond if you are in need. This sense of security contributes to building trust in the relationship.

Trust is promises made promises kept,
consistently over time.

Many times in sessions with couples, one partner becomes distressed. They move to tears, are expressing the hurt or pain they have been struggling with for a while, and in that moment truly become vulnerable. When I see their partner do nothing, often because they have no idea what to do, I see the painful cycle. *If you are in pain, you are on your own.* This painful feeling often perpetuates the cycle between the couple, as there is no relief from the uncomfortable emotions.

Thankfully I get to see it go well too. Sometimes when one partner shares their emotions and becomes vulnerable, perhaps with tears, their partner is able to or knows how to be responsive. That responsive partner reaches out in some way and tries to provide reassurance and relief. Words help, reaching physically helps. You do have to know what your partner typically needs in those moments. You have to be an expert on them and vice versa of course.

One time a husband said, "When I come home and you ignore me, I start to believe you don't want me. It hurts so much." That's a painful thought and feeling to be having. Thankfully in this case it went really well. His wife reached for his hand and said, "Yes. I'm so sorry I do that. I'm sorry I leave you believing I don't want you. I do want you and want to communicate I love you." That's powerful reassurance.

Let me show you how it goes wrong. If the wife had just sat there and didn't respond with reassurance, the husband's distress would have risen. Her lack of reassurance would have validated his fears of not being wanted and left him swimming in a pool of painful thoughts and feelings. When humans experience this, they tend to harden their heart out of self-preservation. The relationship becomes too risky to share thoughts and feelings.

If the situation looks like it could go badly, as a counselor I will step in and ask the quiet partner, in this case the wife, "Is it true that you don't want him?" On very rare occasions the partner says yes, and then we have to deal with where they are at. However, most of the time she'll protest, "No, that's not true at all. I love him. I just don't know how to respond." Then I ask her to offer her hand to her husband and repeat to him what she's just told me. This becomes the response, the reassurance that her distressed husband has longed to hear. Now there is reassurance, relief, and some repair.

Not responding = stonewalling

Blocking or being nonresponsive to someone's needs on purpose is a form of contempt. This is called stonewalling. This is being defiant, evasive, avoidant and refusing to engage. In relationships this communicates, *I will not respond to you. You don't matter to me.* Imagine how well this goes over.

If my wife comes to me and asks for help, I cannot ignore her and expect she'll be okay. If she asks to talk about something important to her, I cannot just say "No" and expect her to continue liking me for very long. Being in a relationship is an unnegotiated contract that says, *I agree to be responsive to you, to protect, soothe, comfort, and support you.* Not responding to someone is a passive yet aggressive approach to expressing one's hurt or anger.

Padding the needle

When I am working with couples, I am always interested in observing the level of responsiveness between them. When one partner is about to say something that might be hard or upsetting to the other, if they are attuned and responsive, they will try to be gentle. When you have to bring up something hard, I suggest you *pad the needle* with words of care.

Padding the needle means offering up compassionate or validating words before you poke them with the needle. "I know you have a hard time when I talk about what happened. Are you okay if I bring it up?" That is preventative repair. It says, "I know this may hurt you. I want you to know that I realize this and want to help you through it." If they say "No," be okay with it for now. Then try again later on. Just be sure and respect their boundary in the moment so they will respect yours in return.

Maybe your partner has been disappointing you lately by not doing much housework; something that you know will be really difficult for them to hear. Padding the needle would be helpful. "I really appreciate you working hard to make sure your job is secure. I want you to know I see that. I see how tired you are when you come home. I was hoping, though, I could ask you to help me keep the house a little neater. Can we talk about that?"

Partners who lack this ability to be responsive will throw their partner under the bus without any leading words of care or compassion. They launch in with "He's such a jerk. He never helps around the house no matter how many times I ask. He just doesn't care."

There is no care in those words, just criticism. Of course, I understand why. This usually happens when the partner who is speaking is desperate for understanding and validation, because their partner is not compassionate or empathetic with them.

A short version of repair is often simply acknowledging what happened and adding an "I'm sorry." When your partner seems hurt, emotional, or in distress, step in with an "I'm sorry sweetheart. I can see you feel I let you down."

You will be expressing empathy and compassion for their experience. These moments happen over and over every day in every couple's life together. When there is a friction point for one, and the other can move in to soothe and repair, the relationship will feel strong and supportive. When partners continually miss these opportunities to strengthen the connection and trust, the relationship suffers.

Step 8

Experiment for This Step

Like other steps in this book, this step requires you to keep
your partner on your radar. You have to pay attention to your
partner's emotions, requests, and needs if you are going to be
responsive to them. As you're doing that, look for chances to
respond to their needs with reassurance.

If your partner makes a request, be responsive by trying
to find a way for it to work for both of you. Hopefully following
this step will increase the level of responsiveness you and
your partner have for each other.

Be more responsive to your partner

This one takes a little mindfulness and a thick skin. Even
if you discuss doing this with your partner, there will be moments you'll grind your teeth. Hang in there; new habits are
hard to form.

When you are interacting with your partner, try to be
more aware of them. If they express an emotion, offer something empathetic in that moment. "Oh, you look upset." If
they make a request, at the very least acknowledge their need
and make sure your partner knows whether you intend to respond and when.

Look for moments to reassure, soothe, and comfort. Be
looking for their emotions and be ready to respond. This way
your partner's emotions won't seem like a surprise. If your

partner seems as though their feelings are hurt, which they might even say to you, step in and offer reassurance. "I'm sorry" can go a long way toward keeping your relationship safe for both of you.

Make a short list of things your partner has expressed they want you to do. Maybe they have asked you to clean the garage or the kitchen. Perhaps they have asked you to hang a picture or put some boxes away. Surprise them by following through. Show that you heard their expressed need. Make it a goal to do one of these per week.

If your partner expresses that they are stressed about a meeting at work, text them just before the meeting and wish them well. Or later, call and say that you hope it went well.

Perhaps they've had a very busy week. Take the kids out to a movie to give them some peaceful time at home.

Notice your partner. If you see they are frustrated, get up and rub their shoulders. Show you notice them and are ready to respond to their distress. Be empathetic.

Affection and sex are *needs,* not wants. If you have been unavailable for sex, acknowledge it and initiate a plan to spend time together.

Help your partner to respond to you

You want to train your partner to treat you better, right? Of course, if you are modeling this as I've just suggested, that will be a great start.

The next step to help them is to make sure *you* are expressing what *you* need. Many of us have a hard time expressing our needs in a relationship. We may not want to be a burden, we might fear getting dismissed or criticized, and we may not think we deserve our needs getting met. These can be legitimate or irrational; either way, remember this—your needs are gifts, not burdens. When you express a need, your partner has a chance to show they love and care. Are you expressing your needs?

Start by expressing small and doable needs. "I need to fix something here, can you help me for a second?" is one. "Would you be able to stop by the store on your way home from work? I need some eggs for breakfast." These requests are expressions of needs. Notice the clear intention.

I realize that expressing a more personal need is also making yourself vulnerable. Yet it is powerful too. This would be something such as asking for support or even a hug. "I had a really tough day today. Can you just sit with me for a few minutes?"

Everyone wants to be wanted. When you express a need in this way you also express that you need and want your partner in return. Moments like this can go well if partners can give each other this clear signal of wanting each other.

What happens if they don't respond?

Remember that you can't blame your behavior on anyone else; you are always responsible for what you say and do. If your partner doesn't hang the picture after you've asked three times, you can't call them a lazy bum. Well, you can, but I'm sure you know how that would go.

To do it right, first make sure you made a request, not a demand, and were clear about your need. If they do not follow through the first time, you can remind them one time. "Hey, are you still going to get to that picture we talked about?"

After you have reminded your partner once (nicely), it is time to switch to curiosity. Don't remind, remind, and remind to the point where you are angry. Instead be curious. Let's say you have already reminded them one time. Now try "We talked about you hanging the picture; my recollection was that you would, but I see you haven't gotten to it." (Nonjudgmental observation.) "I know you're busy." (Validation— letting them off the hook a little.) "I was hoping to get it hung this week and am worried you won't get to it." (Expressing the impact on you.) "Do you need some help, or do you not want to do it now?"

Try to get to the bottom of the issue, don't keep doing the same thing over and over, reminding and reminding, and setting yourself up to become angry.

Chapter Fourteen

Step 9
Cultivate Moments of Connection

*Help your partner continue making <u>the choice</u> to be
with you. Help them feel wanted.*

R emember early on in your relationship when it was really
great? You spent all day excitedly anticipating when you
would see your partner. When you were finally able to reconnect
after all the waiting, they would hug you tight, kiss you with
passion. You didn't want to let go because it felt great to be
wanted! Then when your time together was up, you dreaded having to say goodbye and would procrastinate the moment by
clutching their arm until the last possible second. When they
gave you a big hug goodbye, you felt wanted. It helped you get
through until you saw them again. In time you managed to
weave your lives together. Perhaps you moved in with each other, or maybe you got married. It was relieving to know you were
with them all the time. Now you could snuggle at night and see
them first thing in the morning. It was wonderful to finally be
together. That lasted for a while, at least until life happened.

Busy with work, busy with bills, busy with kids, eventually

the excitement wore off. Now when you are annoyed with your partner and they leave for work you just wave goodbye from the living room. They wave back. When you see each other again, anyone watching might think you're roomies. Upon returning home after being gone all day, does your partner pet the dog and hug the kids before plopping on the couch to watch TV? That's not good. Now perhaps morning snuggles and pillow talk has been displaced with "I gotta get to work." Evening cuddles and check-ins have lost out to the night routine with the kids. Leaving love notes, sending emails that profess your undying love and heartfelt desire, buying flowers, opening the car door, and other romantic gestures have disappeared. "I don't have time" or "I'm too tired" is heard over and over.

In reality, you stop making time. People make time for things that are important to them. So therein lies the problem. *You are not a priority* is now communicated, which hurts. When couples stop doing the things that connected them together and helped maintain closeness, guess what happens? They will stop feeling close and connected. When couples stop treating each other in ways that kept the relationship in that *extra special* zone, the relationship will fall out of that zone and possibly slip down into the *not good enough* zone. If you want to cultivate more closeness and connection in your relationship, you have to do the things that make it extra special by helping your partner feel extra special to you. Do you expect them to always ask for what they need? Sure, that would be great. However keep in mind the following:

We all want to feel wanted,
yet no one likes to ask for it.

164

Thankfully you can fix how it feels to be together with a few small changes in your routine. There are important moments in your daily routine that can do this. They are called *moments of departure* and *moments of reconnection*. Basically these are whenever you leave your partner and whenever you reunite.

Here are some examples of connection building things you can do that are related to leaving and returning.

- Do cuddle in the morning. Don't just get up and leave the bed and sneak out.
- Do say "goodbye" and "I love you" and kiss and hug before leaving the house. Don't wave or salute from the other room.
- Do kiss, hug, talk, or reconnect upon arriving back home. Don't go check your email first.
- Do share the adventures of your day, and ask about theirs. Don't tell them you're too tired to talk.
- Do go to bed at the same time or put your partner to bed if they go earlier. Don't sneak off to bed alone without a "good night."
- Do say good night, hug, kiss, and snuggle before falling asleep. Don't miss the chance to connect with your partner because your eyes are glued to the television.

Getting and staying in sync

Some of the bonding that occurs in childhood happens when children are touched with loving intention. When you were in distress, most likely if someone you trusted would reach out and hold you, your distress would ease. What actually happened when another person physically held you is that the fight-or-flight part of your nervous system was calmed. Your body tension eased because you felt a sense of safety and security from having another person available. You were not alone and to humans, that is powerful anti-stress medicine.

As adults, a real hug is still calming. I am not talking about simply a social shoulder hug, but rather a full body hug held for more than a few seconds. This is physical intimacy; this is communicating, *You are special to me, I value you, I will protect you, and you are safe with me.* We all need this.

A kiss adds intimacy and security. Isn't a kiss a sign of closeness and affection? A peck on the cheek or forehead is nice for your mother, sister or daughter (and the dog), but a kiss on the lips is far better for your partner. It says, *You are special to me, we are close.* Still better is a kiss with some love and passion behind it. A fully body hug along with a romantic kiss during a moment of departure and again upon reconnection can completely change how your day and evening together goes. Try it! This is because it gets your brains aligned after a time apart and then reassured with the idea *We are good, we are secure.*

Confirmation "We are okay"

When you take a moment to check in with your partner before leaving, you are seeking and receiving confirmation *We are okay.* This confirmation provides a deep sense of security that allows you both to calmly go about your day while apart and out of sight of your partner. Upon return, reconnecting with them reconfirms *Yes, we are still okay* and is a critical part of that sense of security. To understand how powerful this is, let me use an extreme example of departure gone wrong. Imagine that just before dropping your child off to school, you tell them, "Have a great day, good luck. Oh, and just so you know, I'm not sure I will be here to pick you up. I might be leaving today. In fact, I may not ever see you again. Have a great day!" Honestly, how do you think their day will go? I am sure you can see how the anxiety from these words would completely disrupt that child's ability to explore, learn, grow, and take risks in their day. Their sense of inner security would be disrupted.

This is not much different from times when a couple has a fight before one has to leave for work and the repair has to wait until the end of the day. Have you experienced how miserable the whole day is when feeling completely disconnected from your partner after an argument? This is partly why those who withdraw as a reaction when in emotional distress make it worse for the other partner. The ambiguity around *Are we all right?* and the anxiety of *What if they give up on me?* have plenty of time to fester and grow. This is not good.

There is a better way to handle departure when you have been fighting and are unable to take time to repair it. The goal is for one of you, ideally the person who seems the angriest (but either will do) to express, *Even though we're fighting, I still love you and want to work this out.* This can work even if you have to take a break because one or both of you is escalating. Think about making this a rule in your household. One of you has to demonstrate love and commitment despite the argument.

When chores, kids, and bills are in the way

I can hear what you're thinking. *How can I stop and hug my partner when the kids are screaming?* That's a fair question because I know those are stressful moments. Let me ask you a question in return. How can you not? Your relationship has to be

167

a priority above all else, except safety, of course. You will never be able to take that ten minutes of quiet time on the couch to hold hands and talk if you do not make it a priority. How can you make this happen? Try organizing the kids in some way. Have a little snack or activity ready, be ready with a short TV show to occupy them, or give them something to do in their room. If those ten minutes with your partner are important, you will figure it out. I am telling you it will be worth it.

I'm not trying to sell you on an hour; I am suggesting that a mere *ten minutes* of reconnecting could change how you both feel in the relationship. You're going to have a really hard time convincing me that you can't figure out how to carve out *ten minutes* to spend with your partner during a critical moment of reconnection. You'll never know unless you try it.

Step 9

Experiment for This Step

Be intentional about connecting with your partner, hugging them, and perhaps adding a kiss, each time either of you leave. Upon return, repeat this and either inquire about their adventures while away or volunteer something about yours. Turn your moments of departure and of reconnection into moments of confirmation that say, *I love you; you are important to me. I want to make sure we're okay.*

Create these key moments

There are several moments of separation that matter each and every day. When you go to sleep at night, when you wake up, when you leave, and when you return. When either of you leaves for more than forty-five minutes (a trip to the store for milk doesn't have to count, though it can!), give the other person a full body hug and kiss. Do this for more than a three-second shoulder hug and more than a peck on the forehead.

When you go to bed, spend a couple minutes snuggling. Or, if one of you is going to bed and the other is staying up, whoever is staying up goes to cuddle for about ten minutes and then tucks the other into bed with a kiss. Yes, just like you would do for one of your children. You want them to have sweet dreams and feel loved and secure, right?

My favorite rule for reconnection at the end of the workday is this—whoever returns home from being away is responsible for seeking out their partner and offering a real hug and kiss. Their partner must stop what they are doing and join them in five to ten minutes of talking and checking in with how each is doing. Next, plan how the evening will look, including when you will spend time together. You will be amazed at how well this works.

Help your partner initiate these moments

Once again, you have to be modeling this with them. As you are doing this, let them know that it feels good for you by pointing it out in the moment. "I really enjoy talking with you." Doesn't that feel good to hear? While you are hugging them say, "I love it when we hug." After a kiss say, "I love kissing you." Or, "I missed you." All these actions and words communicate, *I enjoy being with you.*

After a couple weeks of this, ask them to initiate if they haven't started. You are basically changing a habit in the relationship. Habits take time to break, but this can be done. You are working to create a *new normal* in your relationship.

Chapter Fifteen

Step 10
Love Your Partner *Their* Way, Not Yours

If your partner loves pancakes, don't feed them liver.

In other parts of this book I have talked about ways your communication gets cloudy and what to do about clearing it up. Here, I want to be more direct about how to communicate love in a way your partner will hear and feel. Remember, since everything you do or don't do communicates something and you want to get your partner to respond better to your needs, you first have to motivate them by giving out something they desperately need. They need you to communicate love to them. If you want them to feel extra special and loved, it means communicating love in a way they can hear and feel. Be aware that this might be different than how you hear and feel it.

When we talked about attachment needs I suggested that while we need them all to be met, usually one or two stand out as more important. As part of your work to becoming an expert on your partner, you must become aware of what their key needs are. If you listen to your partner when they are expressing their feelings or acting emotional, you might get some clues. Often in a fight someone will blurt out, "You don't appreciate me." "You don't accept who I am." "You don't understand me." When that happens, they are giving you part of the answer to the question I am asking: what is your partner's key attachment need?

Do you need me?

In working with a couple struggling with a withdrawn partner, there is often a point where I will turn to the partner who seems most eager to fight for the relationship, often the more emotional one, and ask, "Do you believe your partner needs you?"

Typically the answer is "No." Then I ask, "If you don't believe your partner needs you, how can you make sure the relationship survives?" This question usually evokes tears because it brings up the deeper fear and despair that partner is in: the sense of being powerless. If your partner does not need you, you are probably doing the "roommates" thing. Not much of a relationship, is it?

One of the ways this happens in a relationship is when volatility or criticism becomes part of the cycle of communication. When it gets to the point where one of you feels blamed, criticized, and yelled at, that partner will start to believe they will *never be good enough*. They might try, but if the criticism continues, that partner will give up and become distant. Over time, they will become independent to the point where they actually do not need the other. If you're not sharing your needs and meeting your partners you *are* just roommates. Or maybe you're the maid, nanny, or groundskeeper. Either way, this would be sad.

Remember, if your partner doesn't get their need met, for importance, appreciation, acceptance, understanding, or closeness within your relationship, they get emotional. If those emotions don't create action or change from you, reactions emerge. Eventually the final reaction is always distance. If this is happening in your relationship, the dynamic has to change for it to survive.

As a human, you are in the relationship to get your needs met. So is your partner. This is good news because even if you or your partner has gotten to the place of thinking *I don't need you* and has begun living that way, they still do need you. Both of you have those fundamental attachment needs that are connected to emotions. When you meet those needs for your partner, good feelings will follow. If they can get enough of those, better connection can follow. Can it be *enough*? There is no way to tell but by trying.

Of course, you might be in this distant place too, but since you are reading this book I assume you recognize that you need your partner as well. We are all designed to be in relationships, and that means getting needs met. So even if they don't seem to need you, the truth is *they still have those needs*. We just need to rekindle the fire. This means communicating love in a way that evokes good emotions in them. Meeting their attachment needs will do this because remember, *attachment needs activate emotions*. They are part of the same system. You are guaranteed to evoke good emotions in them if you do this, because that is the way we are all wired.

How to be needed

Hopefully by now you've thought about what your partner's top one or two attachment needs are. Are they needing to feel appreciated, accepted, or close? Do they need to be important, be understood, or have you reflect the good in them? If you can choose two, odds are you will hit the target a good percentage of

173

the time. When I was in college I had an economics professor who used to say, "If you're right half the time, you're a genius."

Ask yourself what your partner responds positively to.

- o Do they like it when you <u>tell</u> them how much you love them?
- o Do they like it when you <u>reach for</u> them, to touch them, hold their hand, or cuddle with them? How important is sex to them?
- o Does your partner gush when you buy them a special treat or <u>gift</u>?
- o How about when you clean the house before they get home, or <u>do things</u> for them?
- o Maybe they always complain about not having enough <u>time to spend with you</u>?

Odds are that by mixing one of these types of actions with some expression of their attachment need, you'll hit the jackpot. That means taking some type of action like I have listed above and verbally telling them, "I want you to feel appreciated." Or, "I want you to know you are important to me." When I was in sales we would say, "If you're going to give someone a good deal, it's okay to tell them they are getting a good deal." Underscore it!

For instance, suppose your partner always complains about not being important to you. Maybe they tell you they miss cuddling and being held. Are you listening? They are giving it to you on a golden platter! If you want to communicate love, if you want to be needed by them, *you have to meet their needs with action.* Ask them which night would be good to spend together, rent a movie, and be sure to snuggle up together for the show. Fill their bucket.

Have a difficult or resistant partner?

What if they aren't giving it to you on a golden platter? What if they are really bad at expressing their needs? That does make it tough, but not impossible. If you have been together for a while, most likely you can look at that list of actions above and guess which one fills their bucket o' love.

If you don't know, run some experiments. Each day work on one and note how they respond. Then if they are game, invite them into a conversation about feeling good in the relationship and ask if they noticed any of your actions. If your partner is resistant to the conversation, you might be in a more difficult place than you thought.

A counselor might be helpful. If so, do some research. Don't just pick one who lists "couples" or "marriage counseling" on their website as one of many things they do. Look for someone who publishes their training experience or someone who writes articles on relationships, or ask for referrals from friends or family.

If your partner is resistant to going, visit the resources at www.fixyourpartner.com and look for the "letter to a resistant partner."

Meet their needs their way. Yes, the way they need you to meet them. Sure, it has to work for you too. Motivating your partner to meet your needs means meeting theirs, even if it is awkward or inconvenient. If you want them to prioritize you, you have to prioritize them.

Expressing needs

One reason people fail to get their needs met is simply because they don't ask, or don't ask in a clear way. When you express your needs in a clear way, your partner has a chance to meet that need and thus communicate love. True, they also have a chance to *not* meet the need and communicate you are *not* a priority. Hopefully that isn't what happens.

If your partner is not good at expressing needs, you might have to help. Notice their emotions, put yourself in their shoes, and anticipate what you think they might need or want. This is responsiveness; this is love and care. When you can do this from the place of knowing what their key attachment need is, and let them know you are thinking about them in this way, you will be making major improvements in your relationship.

On the website for this book, there are some free relationship tools you can download. Some of them are designed to facilitate conversations about needs and ways you can work together to improve the relationship. Be sure and visit www.fixyourpartner.com and look for relationship tools.

Taking action as I have suggested in this chapter is really about making your partner's needs a priority. Exactly what you want them to do for you, right?

When I was about to get married, a gentleman pulled me aside and offered some advice I will never forget. Reflecting back on his own marriage of more than twenty years, he said, "We have done well because we prioritize each other's happiness."

To me, I hear, "We are responsive to and prioritize each other's needs." I think the unspoken part is "Even if it is sometimes not what I want to do." Doing this builds the trust and security you both crave.

Step 10

Experiment for This Step

Figure out your partner's two most likely key attachment needs and do something that communicates or responds to those needs. Take steps to meet their need in a way that speaks love to them.

Communicate love *their* way

Thinking about your partner's one or two key attachment needs (if you are not sure, reread chapter three), choose a couple of ways you can meet that need *every day*. When you do, let your partner know.

"I know _____ is important to you, so I _____."
Don't miss the chance to ensure they see your effort!

Sometimes a client and I will strategize a way to better reach their partner. I will suggest they go home and proclaim their intention. Instead the client will take the position of "I'm just going to do it and see if they notice." Ninety-nine point nine percent of the time, when I speak to their partner a week or two later, they will tell me they didn't notice the action. The words reinforce the idea that you are working to be aware, responsive, caring, and willing to take action to show it.

Ask yourself some questions. How can I communicate to my partner that they are important? Appreciated? That I understand what they need, or how they feel? How can I meet their need for closeness and affection? What can I do to communicate that I accept them, warts and all?

These can be little actions such as making them coffee or tea in the morning, packing them a lunch with a love note inside, sending them a text during the day that says, "I love you." You can follow through with something they have been asking you to do. Honestly, just taking time to treat them with some extra specialness or thoughtfulness will work.

The goal here is daily consistency. Small, consistent efforts are easier and more powerful than a big show of love once a year. Anyone can give a gift on their partner's birthday. To express love and care every day is far more powerful.

Help your partner communicate love *your* way

After you have worked on making sure you are meeting their needs for a bit, invite them into a conversation about improving your relationship. Work on expressing a need to your partner in a way they can hear and respond to. Make it a "do," not a "don't." Keep is small and doable. Try to set them up for success.

Frankly, if you are not used to getting love communicated in a way that works best for you, you are just going to have to verbalize it. Let them know about your key attachment needs, request that they make an effort to meet those needs, and help them see how their efforts will impact you, the relationship, and ultimately them. Visit www.fixyourpartner.com and look for the relationship tools link. Download some tools to guide your conversations. Take action and things will change.

Chapter Sixteen

Bonus Step
Follow the Recipe for Love

Love is a verb. You create, cultivate, foster, and build love through actions. The right actions.

What do you think about when I use the word "intimacy"? Do you think of sex? Closeness? Vulnerability? Do you have any of this intimacy in your relationship? When we share intimacy with someone, we become closer, whether it is emotional, physical, or sexual intimacy. The feelings associated with intimacy give us a deep sense of "extra specialness," of connection, vulnerability, trust, and love.

The recipe for love is important to know. If you follow a recipe for a cake once, you'll most likely be able to do it again. The recipe for love is one part talking, one part compassion, and one part touching. This recipe pretty much works with whomever you follow it with, and works even better if they are reciprocating. If you had it with your partner once, you can bake it again.

When you met your partner and began talking and sharing, you offered an increasingly vulnerable side of yourself. As they were compassionate and empathetic toward you, they signaled

179

interest and care. This felt good, right? When your partner shared some of their thoughts and emotions with you and in response you expressed care and concern, you signaled interest and acceptance of them. An emotional bond was created. When you shared and they were compassionate, you probably started to feel connected too.

As you felt this emotional connection growing with your partner, eventually you probably started to think about and long for physical touch. It is a natural outgrowth of the emotional connection and part of what builds a bond. As the emotional connection grew and physical touch was initiated, sex was probably not far behind.

In my practice working with relationships, I see a lot of couples struggling with infidelity. When someone meets another person at the water cooler and over time begins sharing small bits of their emotions and in return gets empathy, compassion, interest, and words that feel supportive, they get a little of what we all crave—understanding. When we share our thoughts and feelings with another person, when we are vulnerable to them, a sense of intimacy and "specialness" grows. Affairs are most often about feeling accepted and understood by someone, while longing for those needs to be met. This creates a connection. The physical component is not usually the primary reason it starts but rather an outgrowth of the desire for increased closeness.

What makes up intimacy?

Intimacy is a deep sense of closeness mixed with vulnerability. When someone is vulnerable with us, we often feel protective of them. When we are vulnerable with someone else and they respond in a way that feels good, a bond between two people is forged. Connection is intimacy and intimacy is connection.

Intimacy consists of three layers:
1. Emotional
2. Physical
3. Sexual

Intimacy means being vulnerable to and with your partner. Vulnerability is a critical component of a happy and secure relationship. To allow yourself to be intimately accepted means putting yourself in a place of being vulnerable. This means allowing them to be there for you. If you (or they) never get into a vulnerable place, you won't establish that deeper connection you long to experience. This means building trust, which happens a little bit at a time by working through these three layers of intimacy.

Emotional intimacy

Emotional intimacy is sharing thoughts and feelings, and this is how it all starts. As I described in previous steps, when you share with your partner what is happening for you emotionally, it helps them get to know you. When you become vulnerable it encourages them to feel and act protective. Doing all this is you letting them inside your world to know you more deeply. Usually this will motivate them to reciprocate and share their world with you. Two people sharing their thoughts, feelings and vulnerabilities is real intimacy. This is two people knowing and updating each other at a deep and private level.

Imagine what happens when one or both partners stop sharing their thoughts, their experiences, and their feelings. The relationship's intimacy takes a hit. You stop feeling as though you know them and start to feel "on the outside," or rejected. When your partner does not talk and share, you naturally conclude that you are not so important or special to them. Now you start to hold yourself back from the relationship. When you hold yourself back or distance yourself, you are not creating intimacy.

Physical intimacy

Physical intimacy is everything physical NOT having to do with sex. Kissing, holding hands, cuddling, hugging, and anything else you might do to reach out and physically connect with your partner that is not intended to signal *I want sex now*. We bond with people we touch with the intention of being compassionate and caring, so touch is a very important need we all have. When we reach out for someone and they respond, the feeling is magical. Emotional and physical intimacy goes hand in hand. If one partner in a relationship does not feel emotionally connected, they may not be open to an offer for physical connection by the other. This can fuel feelings of rejection and a negative cycle.

Let's say you're not feeling emotionally connected. When your partner approaches you for some physical connection such as asking you to cuddle, or kiss, you will probably block their attempt. Since you're not feeling close you probably do not want to communicate that everything is all right. Certainly you don't want to signal that sex is possible. So you block that bid for physical connection and turn away.

This of course leaves your partner feeling rejected, who may become upset or turn away and not repair or try to emotionally connect. Now everyone is hurt and upset. The rejected partner may lash out in response. After becoming vulnerable by expressing their need for closeness and now suffering the hurt of rejection, instead of managing the emotional pain with curiosity, they may well react to that hurt. As you know, reactions won't work.

"Fine! I don't know why I try anyway," they say and stomp out of the room. Of course the rejecting partner feels completely misunderstood since their need for emotional connection wasn't even considered. This fight is all about protesting the disconnection and the fight for closeness.

Physical intimacy is critical. As humans we all need touch. Touch is paramount to the soothing of our stressful lives, the maintenance of our bond. It signals that we are special. We don't need it from every close friend, but we do need it from the critical attachment figures in life. We first had this need from whoever acted as our parent. Later it gets transferred to whoever becomes our romantic partner.

Physical intimacy like kissing and cuddling evokes key chemical reactions in our body that help us feel close, connected, and bonded to our partner. If you are not physical with your partner, the relationship will devolve into just mutual care, which is not enough to sustain most romantic relationships, at least happy and fulfilling ones. Model what you want to create. If your partner is coming up short, let them know your intention is to create more closeness and ask if they'll work on reaching for you more often or in a certain way. If you don't feel emotionally connected, let them know and work on it together. It has to work for both of you, so talk and make a plan together.

Sexual intimacy

Sex is a bonding activity between couples. Your sex life together needs to be nurtured with intention. It has to be tended to just like your house, your job, and your health. A healthy and satisfying sex life helps a couple maintain the extra special bond that can help them stay grounded with each other.

In a relationship where one person wants sex and the other

doesn't, is it okay not to have sex? The answer is "No," because then one partner would be going without their need being met. Unless you have both decided that you are okay without sex, this need is no less important than any other.

When we are going to have sex, we shed our clothing, both real and emotional, and expose our self to the other. Being this vulnerable signals to the other that we think they are special. Even more than that, it says, "I accept you." While this is true for women sometimes, I find that men typically don't talk about their feelings, or ask for the touchy feely stuff, but they do know how to ask for sex. When their partner will have sex, when they will be vulnerable, intimate, and available, what is communicated at some level is that everything is okay. This gives them a huge dose of acceptance.

The touch and affection that one receives from sex are something everyone needs. However, since we are all different, it is important to note that this need can be a higher priority for some. This makes the rejection associated with being pushed away even more painful. This pain is a flood of emotions pulling them in all directions. Anger, sadness, and fear become too much to manage. Coping reactions such as pouting, becoming critical or leaving are common ways people deal with feeling wounded. However, as we have talked about, none of these types of reactionary behaviors will draw the other partner closer again.

When rebuilding connection and intimacy many times men want sex first. The problem is that they don't do the things they need to do to cultivate the emotional connection and closeness the woman needs first. Women, on the other hand, want to stitch their relationship's intimacy back together by starting with emotional connection and closeness.

Either way, someone has to wait and that takes some negotiation. Ideally sex will not be used as a reward or punishment tool for compliance. Willingness and availability to have sex is a sign of connection.

If you love your partner and want to fix the relationship, you can't expect them to meet all your needs before you meet any of theirs. It has to work for both people. Both partners have to have hope that their needs will be met. Otherwise they struggle for motivation.

Negotiating how sex works effectively means that you find a way to make it work for both of you. I realize that this last step in my book can be the most difficult. If having sex is simply the outflow of better emotional and physical connection,

I hope you will be ready after following these steps. If you have a deeper issue such as resentment, lack of trust, or a physical hindrance, I suggest you take steps to work through those issues.

Rebuilding intimacy

Out of all the steps I have offered, this one unfortunately does take some engagement from your partner. You can initiate talking, physical connection, and sex, but it does take some responsiveness on their part to work. Hopefully by the time you get to this step, you and your partner are feeling closer and working together toward more intimacy.

The recipe for love is simple and effective. Connect with someone emotionally, and their desire for closeness with you will grow. Since you have been working through all the steps in this book to communicate better with more love, I am willing to bet your partner is reciprocating more. If so, you both will have stopped doing many of the hurtful things and started doing many of the connecting things. This will be increasing your emotional closeness and most likely lead to welcome chances to be physically and sexually intimate. Even so, let's formulate some experiments so you can actively work to fix your partner and improve your relationship.

Bonus Step

Experiment for This Step

Take action on the concrete steps below to work on your emotional, physical, and sexual intimacy. Be intentional about nurturing your intimate connection on all three levels. Invite your partner to join in on the process. Increased and satisfying emotional, physical, and sexual intimacy, I truly believe, is what keeps the bond between partners strong.

Increase intimacy

Hopefully by following through with all the other experiments in each of the steps, you will already be experiencing better emotional intimacy as well as physical connection and intimacy. In case you haven't, here are some ways to get going more directly.

Emotional connection

During your daily check-in talks or when you are spending time together being close, talk and share your way through these questions. Work through only one question per sitting to get more mileage from this exercise.

1. What types of things can I say to you that make you feel good, wanted, and valued? How does this help you? Give me an example.
2. What are some things you truly struggle with in

your life? Where did these come from in your past? What can I do to be more supportive?

3. When you are upset, how can I help calm you? If you are hurt, how can I help you feel better?

4. What is something that can hurt you that you want to make sure I have on my radar, to make sure I protect you? Where did it come from in your past? How can I do this?

5. What are some things I do that you love and want to make sure I continue?

Physical intimacy

o   Hold hands in the car and whenever you are walking together.

o   Sit next to each other at the restaurant and be sure to touch in some way the whole time.

o   Make sure every day includes a little cuddle time.

o   Snuggle in bed before getting up and before going to sleep.

o   Never leave for more than an hour or return after being apart for more than an hour without a kiss, hopefully more than just an obligatory peck and a hug.

Sexual intimacy

Talk about sex. What do you like, what would you like, how often? Work to be clear on each other's needs and wants.

Visit a lover's shop if you haven't. Even if you don't buy anything, it can be a way to bring fun to the bedroom (or wherever you choose). If you do buy something, know that half the fun is in bringing playfulness to your sex life.

There are more articles on sex on the Internet than you could read in a lifetime. Spend time searching for things that interest you. Ask your partner if they are okay with you sending links to articles that interest you. Now you have things to talk about and experiment with together.

Reigniting your sex life

If you have not been sexually intimate or have issues with how sex goes in your relationship, you might consider going back to school for Sex 101.

First, agree that you will spend time at least once per week, ideally more, on prioritizing sex in your relationship.

To begin getting back in the swing of having sex regularly, break it down. Remember the old bases? You have to get to first base before you can go to second and so on. Start with first base; make sure you both know what the other wants and needs here. It has to work for both of you.

After a few times, go from first to second. As you are comfortable go from first to second and then third. Finally, first, second, third, and home. Move on when each of you agrees and is ready. Remember, you are rebuilding emotional and physical intimacy.

First base is cuddling and kissing with clothing on. This is in bed, on the couch, or wherever is comfortable. Later, talk together about how it felt.

Second base is touching with loose clothing, or no clothing, but no genital touching. On the bed, couch, or where you are comfortable. Follow up later with a talk about how it felt.

Third base is still more touching, clothing optional, and

includes some genital touching, but is not limited to that. Use what you have learned about each other during the first two steps. Later, spend time talking about what you liked and how it felt.

Home base is erotic touching. Manual, oral, vibration, etc., to the point of feeling aroused or even orgasm for one or both. Home base should include all these things you have learned and includes intercourse. Orgasm is not limited to intercourse. It might be through oral sex or stimulation of some kind. Most of all, keep talking about all this and make it part of the extra special emotional connection you share.

Help your partner succeed

With regards to intimacy, you would most likely want your partner to initiate it at least some of the time. You want them to want to talk with you and hear about your day. You want them to reach for you physically, so you can feel wanted. You want them to want you sexually.

Once again, modeling all this with them as suggested above will help you set the stage for your request, which is for them to initiate all these types of intimacy. Then invite them to a conversation about your sex life together and let them know how important it is to you that they make an effort to initiate.

Chapter Seventeen

The Fruit Awaits!

As a man, a father, a husband, a son, and as a professional who works with individuals and couples, I deeply hold the belief that our purpose in life is to love and be loved. Being in a secure, loving relationship with another who we trust to be there for us is the greatest of life's joys.

I myself have experienced, and see on a daily basis, the struggle we all have when our relationships no longer work. When we cannot trust, when we feel alone, when we don't have the security of someone watching our back, everything in life becomes hard. As humans, we need the security a close and safe relationship brings, to give us the solid footing we need to step out and conquer the world. If we don't have it, we feel alone and become stuck.

My goal in writing this book is to be a catalyst of change. I want to help facilitate your efforts to build your relationship into an extra special one. *Fixing your partner* means being intentional about meeting your partner's needs. It means expressing that you value your partner, so that they value you and in return want to meet your needs. I hope by following these steps you have achieved significant progress toward that goal, from whatever point you started.

Throughout our lives we go through developmental stages.

As such, we are constantly changing, which forces our partner to change as well. This means our relationship is a continually evolving entity. Our relationship must be nurtured, fed, soothed, protected, comforted, and cherished, just like our partner. I believe that using all the steps I have outlined in this book will give you the tools necessary to do this, to make sure your relationship thrives.

I leave you now with a listing of my favorite statements sprinkled throughout this book and a few others that I offer. These form a solid framework of relationship values that will guide you and help build the secure and loving relationship you crave.

Thank you for letting me share my thoughts, theories, and beliefs for improving relationships. Write me after you have tried applying these steps and let me know how it goes.

Marlon-isms

Here are all the sound bites from the book, along with a few of my favorites that aren't, all in one place. These are "rules to live by" that I have accumulated from various sources during my time working as a counselor. For all those who have contributed, thank you!

- o Everything we do or don't do communicates something.
- o We hang around people who help us feel good about our self.
- o When you react, you always get the opposite of what you want.
- o You cannot blame someone else for your own behavior.
- o We know ourselves by our intentions; we know others by their actions and words.

- Lead with your intention and you'll have a better chance of getting what you want.
- No one likes to be told what to do.
- Any moment of correction has the potential of being criticism.
- There are no demands in relationships, only requests.
- You don't have to accept every invitation to fight. Learn how to decline with grace.
- Criticism is *never* okay in a relationship with someone you love.
- The phone rings both ways. Go talk to your partner first.
- Trust is promises made, promises kept consistently over time.
- We all want to feel wanted, but no one likes to ask for it.
- Your needs are gifts to your partner, not burdens. It's how they know to express love.
- Love is a verb. Love is what you do.
- Connection = Validation + Empathy.
- Feeling understood is the path to connection.
- You can't change it unless you own it.
- Being Right has no place in a close relationship.

Chapter Eighteen

What to Do for More Help

Nothing is impossible. Some things just take more work.

In writing *Fix Your Partner in 10 Easy Steps or Less!* I have worked to select the ten best steps you can take. My goal is for them to be concrete and doable steps that lead you to a happier and more secure relationship with your partner. Hopefully these ten steps have become small changes you have been making on the road to feeling closer and more connected. I absolutely and truly believe that each and every step is a critical one to take and will lead to positive results. So if you have not experimented with them, what are you waiting for? I do acknowledge that some partners and couples might need more guidance and ideas than any book can offer. That's why I want to let you know where you can find even more support for your relationship.

www.fixyourpartner.com

At www.fixyourpartner.com you will find several additional resources designed to support your efforts to have a relationship that isn't just "good enough," but rather one that is extra special. You will find tools and resources to help with all the key areas of your relationship that might need attention. Visit the book's site and you can . . .

- ○ Receive my free guide to deciding if your relationship is worth fixing.
- ○ Learn how to be an expert on your partner so you both can feel more secure.
- ○ Create a "rules of engagement contract" to help increase emotional safety.
- ○ Learn how to play the "gratitude game" to feel better more often.
- ○ Sign up for my free newsletter to help you assess the relationship and life areas that may be what is causing hurt feelings and conflict in your relationship.
- ○ See an example of a letter you can write to try and get a resistant partner to attend counseling with you.

Professional counseling

When you are working to consciously and intentionally improve your relationship, professional marriage or relationship counseling can be helpful. Having someone who is outside of your emotions and who understands the process of relationships can help you and your partner navigate the rough rapids that are in your way. All the steps, resources, tips, and tools I am offering can still support any work you would do in counseling, alone or with your partner. Yet, for big issues that you are having trouble navigating, don't hesitate to look for a counselor to help.

If you are thinking of searching for a relationship counselor, visit www.fixyourpartner.com and receive my special report on how to choose the right counselor for you. You will learn...

o   How to locate counselors in your area.

o   What types of counselors are available and how to tell them apart.

o   The different types of methods you might encounter, which are okay and which to avoid.

o   The questions to ask to determine if the counselor is qualified.

o   How to help the counselor help you.

If you are committed to your relationship and your partner, but have struggled to help your relationship improve, my goal is that by reading this book you have found some hope for a better relationship. I wish you the best in your efforts to build a secure and loving relationship and receive the love you deserve.

Having a Hard Conversation

Paramount to having a solid long term relationship is your ability to talk about stormy issues and reach calmer waters. Since many hard conversations are going to be about someone needing to make a course correction, you have to have a way to navigate them. Let's talk about how to initiate and have that hard conversation, so you can get back on course together.

Step 1   Issue an invitation

If I were to walk up to my wife and say, "We really need to talk about the money you're always spending." I have no doubt that she would feel blindsided and criticized. Putting her on the defensive right from the start isn't going to help her be compassionate to what I want out of the conversation.

If you are the one needing to have a talk, you'll do better to take responsibility for communicating your needs in a way your partner can take in. Using words, body language and a tone that is inviting is all helpful stuff. Start by asking them if they will talk and when it works best for them. Give them a choice by making it a request or invitation conveys freedom, which means there is less for them to resist. Start with something like, "Hey, I would like to talk about how we argue with each other. When would you be willing to talk about that?"

197

"I really need to talk about what happened last night. When can we do that this morning?"

"Do you have time to talk about our finances today? Can we do that after diner or before bed?

Notice how in the last one I suggested two choices. If you find they put off the conversation, offer two choices.

Step 2   State your intention

Whenever you hear, see or experience something, your brain is going to calculate how it will impact you. When you walk up and invite your partner, their brain is going to factor in how conversations usually go, how difficult the topic is and how up for it they feel. Offering your intention can soften the walls their brain might be building.

"My intention is for us to agree on some rules so we can disagree without all the fighting."

"My intention is to repair things, so we can feel more connected again."

"My intention is for us to get on the same page with how we spend money, so we can both feel good."

These help your partner feel better about the end goal for having the conversation. It answers the question we all ask at a deep level: "What's in it for me."

Step 3   State what you observe without judgment

When you open the conversation, it is helpful to restate your intention. Then take a moment to explain what you are seeing or experiencing that is an issue for you. When you do this, it is very important that you do so without judgment. No absolutes like "you always" or "you never". No belittling, criticizing, sarcasm or blaming. Instead, talk about what you *notice*. Consider that where possible, it helps to use "we" instead of "you".

"I notice that when we argue, we sometime use words that are hurtful to each other."

"I noticed last night you came home after midnight which was two hours after you had originally said. I also noticed that I hadn't gotten a call or text to let me know.

"I noticed that the bank account was overdrawn two times last week."

Stating your observations this way can go a long way to avoid putting your partner on the defensive.

Step 3   Pad the needle with validation

Everyone needs validation. Offering validation will help them tolerate the conversation and stay engaged. Since this is a hard conversation, most likely there will be a needle in it for them somewhere. Before you stick the needle, offer a little padding to ease the pain.

"I know that you don't like how we argue and yell at each other either."

"I know you like to go out with your friends and not worry too much about time."

"I know you work hard to manage the money for us."

These little statements of validation can make a huge difference when it comes to them staying engaged and collaborative or not. It can ease any sense of being either blamed or feeling as though you are saying they are not good enough.

Step 4 Make your request

Finally, make your request of them. This is best framed as a favor. For this to be effective it has to feel like a choice. You want them to feel free to be in the relationship and to work on being their best self. If you use ultimatums, demands or orders, it will probably backfire if not immediately, in the long run.

"It would help me out if when we start to argue and escalate, we could agree to back away for a bit and let things cool."

"Would you be willing to make an agreement about how to manage things when you are going to be out later than you agree and how to keep in touch so I do not worry."

"I would really like it if you would work with me on how we make decisions to spend money."

When someone feels hurt

As you have read in the chapters about emotions and reactions, when someone feels hurt they may become defensive or attacking. If that happens, it only takes one of you to hang on and not fall into that trap. A quick repair attempt can keep the train on the tracks.

In response to a jab try, "That's not helpful right now." Or, "Can we please not do that to each other right now?"

In response to your partner becoming defensive or realizing you jabbed them, say "I'm sorry, that wasn't very nice of me to say."

Or try, "I'm sorry if I said something that hurt your feelings."

Or say, "Yes, I did just poke you. I'm sorry. I appreciate you talking with me. I will work harder not to do that."

Throughout this book I have offered ways to communicate that bring rules of engagement, safety, soothing, compassion, empathy and repair to your relationship. As you navigate a hard conversation, all those same rules apply.